CRAZY FOURTH

CRAZY FOURTH

How Jack Johnson Kept His Heavyweight Title and
Put Las Vegas, New Mexico, on the Map

Toby Smith

University of New Mexico Press | Albuquerque

Library of Congress Cataloging-in-Publication Data
Names: Smith, Toby, 1946– author.
Title: Crazy Fourth: how Jack Johnson kept his heavyweight title and put
Las Vegas, New Mexico, on the map / Toby Smith.
Description: Albuquerque: University of New Mexico Press, 2020. |
Includes bibliographical references and index.
Identifiers: LCCN 2019040607 (print) | LCCN 2019040608 (e-book) |
ISBN 9780826361431 (paperback) | ISBN 9780826361448 (e-book)
Subjects: LCSH: Johnson, Jack, 1878–1946. | Flynn, Jim, 1879–1935. |
Boxing—New Mexico—Las Vegas—History. | Las Vegas (N.M.)—History.
Classification: LCC GV1132.J7 S65 2020 (print) | LCC GV1132.J7 (e-book) |
DDC 796.83092 [B]—dc23
LC record available at https://lccn.loc.gov/2019040607
LC e-book record available at https://lccn.loc.gov/2019040608

Cover photograph courtesy of Annie Leonard
Designed by Felicia Cedillos
Composed in Goudy Oldstyle Std 10.25/14.5

En memoria de Johnny Tapia

All Hail!
How the fire will fly
On the Fourth of July;
How the cannon and crackers will rattle!
Mr. Fireman Flynn
Will endeavor to win
From the "Smoke" in the championship
battle.
How the rockets will soar
And the fireworks roar
'Til the din on the atmosphere lingers!
Mid excitement intense
In the course of events
Little Willie will blow off his fingers.
Hip, hip, and hooray
For the glorious day!
We will make a national mirth day,
Mid tumultuous toots
We will fire salutes
On our hundred and thirty-sixth birthday!

—L. C. DAVIS, POET LAUREATE–SPORTING WRITER,
St. Louis Post-Dispatch, July 2, 1912

CONTENTS

INTRODUCTION

On an agreeable June afternoon in 1994, I set off for Las Vegas, New Mexico. As the proprietor of a weekly sports column for the *Albuquerque Journal*, I had been thinking for a good while of writing something about a big prize-fight that little Las Vegas staged back in 1912.

This was the world heavyweight boxing championship in which the reviled—and to a much lesser degree revered—Jack Johnson took part. Johnson was the first African American to occupy what then was the loftiest throne in all of sportsdom. His appearance that Fourth of July more than a century ago remains the only world heavyweight title bout to occur in New Mexico. In all likelihood, there will not be another anytime soon and, certainly, not one like the first.

Whenever I drive north on Interstate 25, I am frequently surprised to see Las Vegas suddenly appear as if it had been waiting to do business on the west side of the highway. Meanwhile, directly to the east a prairie-grass panorama lies undisturbed, as if pondering in silence its emptiness.

Eventually that afternoon I found the newspaper office of the *Las Vegas Optic*, where I asked a woman for any information on the fight. Rummaging about for several minutes, she could not locate clippings. "What about microfilm?" I suggested. She told me the newspaper's microfilm reader was on the fritz and recommended I go over to the New Mexico Highlands University library. Her directions were spot-on.

The microfilm apparatus in the library was the antiquated kind. It required sticking your head into a cave-like opening of a metal box and reading blurry type while cranking a handle. To understand such a device, try to imagine the last time you peered into your fireplace to see if the damper happened to be closed.

From a 1912 reel of film I read articles about the training camps of Johnson and his opponent, Jim Flynn, and how many thousands of people were expected to attend the prizefight. One story said that the event might not even be held.

There were photographs, too, and one striking picture I remember well. It was of Jack Johnson wearing his Sunday best and sitting on the front porch of a house in Las Vegas. His face was dark, its features barely visible. Alongside him was his white wife in a dress the color of fresh flour. The couple stared at the camera, their boredom almost palpable.

After three hours or so of microfilm squinting, I went to get something to eat. When I finished, dusk had begun to creep over Las Vegas, and I decided to start for home. At the south end of Grand Avenue, a neon sign suddenly grabbed my attention. The sign stood atop a bunker-like, white stucco building and it said Joe's Ringside Inn.[1]

My foot couldn't hit the brakes fast enough.

I had heard that the Johnson-Flynn fray had been something of a zany mishmash from the get-go, weeks before it actually took place. If I wanted to find out more about the fight, I sensed that this tavern might offer something besides a beer.

Joe Roybal had been the original owner of the bar, his niece Yolanda Arellanes told me that night as we talked inside the Ringside's smoky confines. Born in Mora County, New Mexico, in the year before the Las Vegas fight, Joe grew up an attentive student of the sweet science. As a young man—this being the late 1920s and early '30s—he participated in some amateur fights and considered himself pretty tough.[2] That was until he squared off against a formidable young black foe. Yolanda said her uncle told her, "Guy hit me so hard I didn't want to box no more."

Soon after that, Joe started promoting regional fights, a much healthier vocation than getting smashed in the face. During one of the fight cards Joe put together in Arizona, he met his wife-to-be, Gloria Valencia. They married in Bisbee, Arizona, and settled in Las Vegas, New Mexico. Boxing has a long history in San Miguel County and Joe Roybal had a ringside seat for much of the action.

In 1943, when the army ordered Joe into uniform, he closed the Ringside. When the war ended, Joe and Gloria relocated to the other Las Vegas, the one in Nevada, where Joe worked for a time as a casino pit boss. The couple returned to New Mexico in 1947 or '48, Yolanda said.

Soon enough Joe opened the Ringside Inn, at the southern approach to

Las Vegas. That's the joint I walked into in 1994. The lounge prospered as a popular hangout for all sorts: county laborers right off the job and their lady friends. Devotees of Friday Night Fights on the TV above the bar. Those in attendance might include sunburned vaqueros, slaphappy palookas, and everyday folks seeking a night out or hoping to meet up with a pal or three.

Put simply, Joe's Ringside was a good place to nurse a cold Pabst and shoot the bull. Short and pugnacious, Joe greeted patrons with a quick wave, an ever-present cigar between his teeth, and a cowboy hat on his head. Joe could be businesslike. He held tight to every nickel that came his way. He did not, however, lack a sense of humor. Sentences that came from Joe's mouth did not end with a period but with the laugh of a cackling crow.

"A showman" is how Yolanda put it.

The Ringside was many things but most of all it was a boxing hangout. Joe hired an artist, whose name has been lost to time, to paint a mural on one wall that depicted the rowdydow that Johnson had in Las Vegas in 1912 with Fireman Jim Flynn, a vinegary sort who grew up around the steel mills of Pueblo, Colorado.

From an early age, Joe had heard tales about that fight, Yolanda said. Joe was at work in a local grocery store one day in the 1920s when a dark stranger dressed to the nines appeared in the doorway. It was the Big Smoke himself, Joe soon realized. John Arthur Johnson, Jack to everyone. Already he was the most famous black man on earth.

Ever the comic, Joe quickly took on the nasally voice of a ring announcer: "And in this corner . . . in the black trunks . . . weighing 220 pounds . . . the world heavyweight champeen."

Johnson, who was in town to visit an old friend he had made in 1912, whooped with approval. "Son," the eminent pugilist said, "you ought to think about doing that for a living." This time it was Joe's turn to hoot. His living, it turned out, was Joe's Ringside.

In the early 1970s a fire struck the bar and destroyed the taproom's mural. Shortly after that, Joe contracted another mural, which also depicted the Johnson-Flynn bout. Wilfred Salazar painted that version.

As it aged, the Ringside gained an unsavory reputation. Known gamblers took up residence in a back room, with high-stakes card games and craps on the agenda.[3] At intervals, traveling strippers paraded their stuff. Wrestling matches commenced on the Ringside's floor. And then there was the bear, a real, live, honest-to-goodness *Ursus arctos*.[4]

A fellow brought the animal into the place on a leash one night and took bets on anyone who was brave enough—or rattle-brained enough—to tangle with the creature. In time brawls erupted with regularity at Joe's and there was even a shooting.

Getting on in years and ailing, Joe could no longer keep order. He asked his niece to take over the business. Joe and Gloria did not have children; Yolanda was like a daughter. Serene and polite, Yolanda could not see herself managing such a gutbucket. Joe begged and pleaded until Yolanda finally agreed. She cleaned up the Ringside, bid adieu to the bad apples, and supervised a series of renovations.[5]

Regrettably, the wall that served as home for the second mural of the Johnson-Flynn fight met with the blows of a sledgehammer. Joe Roybal's knockabout life ended September 6, 1993, in a Las Vegas nursing home. He was eighty-two years old. Yolanda eventually gave up the Ringside and moved to Albuquerque.[6]

I didn't learn too much about Johnson and Flynn that day in 1994, except that I wanted to know more. In the subsequent years I kept a growing stash of relevant bits and pieces connected to the encounter, including a DVD of the fight that I made from an eight-millimeter movie I purchased online.

A good many of those items were amusing in content. Indeed, the proceedings heading toward July 4, 1912, seemed dominated by ludicrous incidents and rare-bird characters. The star character, of course, being Jack Johnson.

That the iconic Johnson spent almost three weeks in New Mexico lured me from the beginning. And yet Johnson's very presence in the state once upon a time often comes as a surprise to others. Indeed, even some natives of long standing, I learned, knew nothing of Johnson's stay or of the world championship.

Confusion surrounding the fight continues to this day. Some people, even a few who dwell in the city of Las Vegas, believe the fight took place where the remains of the Joe's Ringside still stand. As natural as that thought might seem, it is untrue. The fight occurred at what was then the far north end of the community.

Meanwhile, there are those people who were aware Johnson had defended his heavyweight crown in Las Vegas, but were fairly sure that defense occurred in the Las Vegas that sprawls in the flats of Nevada. However, any prizefighting done in dusty, sparsely populated Las Vegas, Nevada, in 1912, likely transpired without gloves and beneath the roof of an ungentlemanly, whiskey-sloshing saloon.

Some individuals, even a few New Mexicans, mistakenly believe the 1912 fight was the basis for the 1969 movie (and earlier a Pulitzer Prize–winning stage play) *The Great White Hope*. Jim Flynn was clearly a White Hope but not *the* Great White Hope. That honor belonged to Jim Jeffries, two years earlier. In the play and in the movie, Johnson showed up in Reno, Nevada, with a white girlfriend (his wife, in real life).

Not knowing the particulars of the New Mexico meet-up is easily forgiven. There exist some worthy articles about it, but many of those are understandably condensed. Original sources, such as people who witnessed the sideshow that Las Vegas became following the announcement of the bout in January 1912—and their number was small to begin with—long ago went to the last roundup. Details now turn up chiefly in microfilm of old newspapers and magazines, and in a scattering of books.

By the time Johnson reached Las Vegas, he was a man in full. After 1912, Johnson remained in the fight game for a long spell, if not always at the top tier. He continued to make news in and out of the ring unceasingly, it seemed, for decades. He had cameos in moving pictures, joined the cast of burlesque shows on Broadway, spent almost a year in a federal prison, traveled the vaudeville circuit, and had six different wives—four of them white. Earlier, he had wed two black women. When those unions fell apart, he forswore black women forever.

At various times he ran a saloon in Tijuana, a nightclub in Chicago, and another hangout in Los Angeles. For a while he trained as a bullfighter. He kept the company of some of his era's most desired women, including German spy Mata Hari and sex symbols Lupe Velez and Mae West. Deep into his retirement, Johnson continued to pop up in headlines for the smallest of reasons. He did not enter into his golden years quietly. He battled the ugliest forms of racism his entire life, including in his very last hours.

Johnson did not always behave well. To paraphrase the manager of heavyweight boogeyman Sonny Liston, a part-time penitentiary resident and a full-time heroin addict, Jack Johnson had a lot of good points. It was his bad points that weren't so good.[7]

The record book shows that, beginning in 1902, Johnson had nearly eighty professional fights in his lifetime. There were also numerous exhibitions, feats-of-strength performances, and rambling discourses at Hubert's Flea Circus, on New York City's gritty Forty-Second Street and Broadway. In April 1942 Johnson appeared with a freak troupe in downtown Denver. On the marquee with him was Athelia the Monkey Girl, Zaza the Alligator Girl, and Eko and Iko, sheep-headed fellows from the wilds of Ecuador.

Much like Joe Roybal, Johnson loved an audience. Frequently he would take the spotlight to crack jokes or give opinions, but mostly he jabbered on at length about his favorite subject—himself. Now and then he would pause to sip red wine through a straw.

Unforgivable Blackness, Ken Burns's splendid documentary about Johnson, runs just short of four hours. That the PBS production gives the Johnson-Flynn showdown in New Mexico only eighty seconds is testimony to the full-of-beans existence Jack Johnson left behind.

Over time, three autobiographies bearing Johnson's name were published, though clearly all were collaborative efforts in large part. In only one of those life stories is his July 1912 meeting with Jim Flynn mentioned, and that covers but a single paragraph. Books about Johnson are numerous. One of those tomes, published in 1927, comes with five different forewords, which has to be a book-publishing record.

On no shelf will you find a Jim Flynn book. A respectable fighter who endured 133 clashes in the ring, Flynn's personality out of the ring was that of a pit bull with a sore foot.

The *Encyclopedia of World Biography* offers a detailed account of Johnson's time on Earth. However, not one word is given to what took place long ago in Las Vegas, New Mexico.

A doorstop-like compendium titled *The Leading Facts of New Mexican History*, marshaled by the eminent historian Ralph Emerson Twitchell, reveals zero facts about the fight. Do such shortcomings make the beleaguered affair inconsequential? On the contrary, the 1912 contest is of pronounced significance for several reasons.

The fight offers a bridge between two of Johnson's most memorable hours in a boxing ring. In 1910, in Reno, Nevada, also on the Fourth of July, Johnson pummeled into submission a national treasure and the most acclaimed of all White Hopes, Jim Jeffries, in what was then called the "Fight of the Century."

At the urging of White America, which at the time abhorred the idea of a black fighter laying claim to the most glittering crown in all of athletics, Jeffries had been pressed into a comeback. Slow afoot, weary of arm, the champion known simply as Jeff was not up to the task. He had retired from the ring unblemished in 1905, and his distaste for Johnson was widely and openly shared.

Johnson was a réclame whose roving eye typically came to rest upon white women. He married a quartet of them, to America's horror.[8]

That Johnson tossed around folding money as if flipping bread crumbs into a duck pond irked every grade of society. What is more, Johnson strutted about in the haberdashery of a Beau Brummell and drove lead-footed everywhere, always in the newest and snappiest motor cars.

In 1915, in Havana, Cuba, on a blazing April afternoon, Jess Willard, clumsy yet country strong, wore down the rusty champion Johnson over twenty-six rounds. Willard scored a knockout, as Johnson so often had done to others in the ring.

Much like Jeffries in Reno, Johnson was beyond his heyday and unprepared. A roll of flesh from the good life abroad circled the man's midsection. Even so, Johnson saw the oafish Kansan as one more lubberly Caucasian attempting to knock the world's best down a peg. That exhausting confrontation ended, for all intents and purposes, Johnson's boxing career. To the satisfaction of millions in the United States, prizefighting's most honored achievement returned to a white man.

Johnson had grabbed boxing's greatest diadem in 1908 by chasing after Tommy Burns, the reigning heavyweight conqueror, with monomaniacal fervor, and traveling to Australia. There Johnson dallied with Burns, a Canadian bigot with skin paler than Jim Jeffries's. The 1912 bout would become the last time Jack Johnson stood on American soil as the supreme monarch of all heavyweight combatants.

The fight in Las Vegas, New Mexico, has additional meaningfulness because, almost a month afterward, Congressional lawmakers passed a bill prohibiting the interstate transportation of prizefight films. No sensible person wanted to see a repeat of the terrible fallout that followed the Johnson-Jeffries clash: a black man giving an esteemed white man a thorough thrashing in the boxing ring, an outcome that sparked repellent race riots. The new law, which led to the bootlegging of fight films through the years, was finally abolished in 1939.[9]

To many US citizens, the New Mexico bout was an acquaintance, through newspaper and magazine accounts and newsreels, with the West. The Johnson-Jeffries set-to in Reno, Nevada, in 1910, had brought the West into clear focus. Still, New Mexico was not all wild and woolly as many likely imagined, but was quite civilized. Indeed, misconceptions abounded.

The vast vacant spaces of the state of New Mexico—which only six months before the fight had been a territory—were not part of Mexico, as extensively presumed and written as a certainty by journalists assigned to cover the contest. This was definitely not America's heartland. Nor was this shiny-new member of statehood filled with savage Indians, though it did have a sizable population of cowboys, many of whom resided close by Las Vegas. The Las Vegas in New Mexico, that is.

Las Vegas, New Mexico, was instead well civilized in 1912, thanks to the railroad, which had begun to hiss and steam and finally pull up there in 1879.

Of further importance, Johnson's meeting with Flynn that Independence Day presaged two of the saddest moments in the champion's very public life. The suicide of his first white wife, who had accompanied him to New Mexico, came just two months after the Las Vegas fight. That tragedy was soon followed by a hasty marriage to another white woman, clearly one more bothersome point for Johnson critics, of whom there were then many. That second marriage helped to move forward the US government's charge that Johnson had violated the little-used Mann Act, a morals law upheld for the sole purpose of putting Johnson behind bars.[10]

The threat of imprisonment caused the world champion to flee the country and reside in exile in Europe for what became three years.

In some ways it is amazing that the 1912 fight gained any attention at all, eclipsed as it was by more momentous happenings in the world. Less than three months before the fight, the RMS *Titanic* was sailing gaily along on its maiden voyage when it struck a mountainous slab of ice. That mistake sent more than 1,500 people to their deaths in the frigid North Atlantic. Stories about the *Titanic* grabbed prime space in newspapers—then the country's principal news source—for weeks, even in some papers on the day of the fight.

Concurrently, political upheaval in the United States provided a contentious backdrop for 1912. On through the prizefight until November, party conventions and electioneering continued to rate king-sized headlines, extensive reportage, and in many cases, every inch of a paper's editorial page. The seriousness of several 1912 happenings can be balanced that year by the joyous surprise of finding tiny toys for the first time inside boxes of Cracker Jack.

Incumbent president William Howard Taft had seemed a shoo-in to remain in office. Such a feeling lasted until the ego-driven Theodore Roosevelt, once Taft's good friend, stepped in to form his own Republican coalition, the progressive Bull Moose Party. The GOP split proved so divisive that Woodrow Wilson, a Democrat, came forward to win the election and become the twenty-eighth president.

The Johnson and Flynn joust was not even the most exciting prizefight on July the Fourth of 1912. In Vernon, California, over thirteen rounds, Ad Wolgast and Joe Rivers battled each other for possession of the world lightweight title. The two men fooled each other by landing simultaneous knockout punches. In Las Vegas, Johnson and Flynn simply fooled around in the ring.

The other Las Vegas, the one in Nevada, will forever be known as the boxing venue that led Mike Tyson into a fit of monstrous lunacy on a June evening in 1997. Tyson masticated part of Evander Holyfield's right ear. If that incident provided the most bizarre conclusion to a world heavyweight championship, the 1912 Johnson-Flynn mashup definitely falls in the ranks of the runners-up.

The New Mexico fight is worthy of excavation because the whole affair reeked of ineptitude. Any historic consequences the championship carries were equaled by the preposterous goings-on around it. The ninety-some days preceding the world title bout in New Mexico frequently seemed an early-day version of *The Gong Show*, that absurdist television program of the 1970s. Long ago a gong, in boxing terminology, had the same role as today's bell. A prizefight gong was a hard disc that a timekeeper or ring announcer struck with a hammer. The clangorous sound that followed could rouse King Tut.

The Johnson camp turned into an unending series of shenanigans, day after day, with very little training taking place. Meanwhile, at Flynn's camp, turmoil seemed almost like a daily episode. The main event was stopped— not by the referee but by an officious, badge-wearing lawman, who had nearly fallen on his face while climbing into the ring. That man had no business being there in the first place. He was abetted by a clueless governor who didn't bother to attend the fight in his own backyard because he didn't want it to transpire.

For the nine rounds their fight barely lasted, Johnson and Flynn resembled prize buffoons rather than prizefighters. This was, to be sure, not a pulse-pounder. It was comedic relief, and clowns were sent in. The referee was a Johnson chum, a sports editor from Chicago who, during the rests between gongs, looked as if he were making notes—mental and otherwise—for his newspaper column that would run the following morning.

The fight's press agent was an ex-newshound who could hustle hot dogs to a pig farmer. His Barnum-like promises surely suckered readers and news writers across America into believing the event would be a Roman gladiatorial spectacle witnessed by tens of thousands of frothing onlookers.

The promoter of the fight, Jack Curley, was a corn-silk-smooth operator from San Francisco whose real future, it turned out, was putting forth wrestling matches for the public. During the spring of 1912, instead of taking care of this heavyweight championship fight, the event's matchmaker revealed himself to be a heavyweight cad. He got into nearly as many jams with women as the insatiable eighth overlord of England. Meanwhile, instead of training for the contest, Johnson took joyrides in his motorcar, or played the bass viol, or rolled dice deep into the night with his sparring partners.

That left Flynn to eat everything in sight at his base camp only to watch his head trainer quit on the spot in exasperation two weeks before the fight. The camps of both boxers became minidramas featuring the strangest casts and goings-on to ever decorate the fringe of a major sporting experience. Blame for the championship's piddling attendance and its miserable performance was passed around everywhere. Viewed today, the entire scenario reveals a baffling display not of athletic deftness but of absolute daffiness.

When the two antagonists were not dumbly lurching about the ring in each other's clutches, Johnson latched onto an amused expression while Flynn took flight—literally. Even to the untrained eye, the two principals acted as if they had never boxed a round in their lives. It is such attendant folly that helps to define the 1912 fight—before, during, and after. As the saying goes, you can't make up this stuff.

What would old Joe Roybal do if he got wind of all these cockamamie elements? I suspect he would remove his cowboy hat and scratch his naked scalp. "That ain't boxing," Joe might say. Odds are good he might bust an abdominal laughing. With that, he would likely laugh some more.

CHAPTER I

Birth of a Debacle

HOW DID SUCH a sporting calamity come into being? Or, as the chicken farmer yawped to his missus: "Who laid this rotten egg?" Late one luminous afternoon in Paris, during the summer of 1911, Jack Curley, a moon-faced fellow with a bad haircut, was strolling to his hotel when he caught sight of Jack Johnson on the Champs-Élysées.[1] Curley was in Paris to tour with a wrestler named "Doc" Roller who, believe it or not, was a licensed physician.

Professional wrestling in those days was real. Curley at that time specialized in the promotion of grappling matches. He had gained nationwide prominence as the promoter behind the Gotch-Hackenschmidt exhibitions, then a frenziedly popular means of entertainment.

Taller and darker than a great many people, Johnson was hard to miss that afternoon. He was, after all, the most celebrated man of color on the planet. For this enjoyable July the Fourth, which coincidentally happened to be Jack Curley's birthday, anything seemed possible.

Johnson apparently had been celebrating the holiday. The two men, who knew each other some, stopped for a few minutes to natter on about nothing, at least nothing that could be of historic significance.

When that conversation ceased, the pair went their separate ways. Curley, however, couldn't get the idea out of his head that Johnson might be interested in another prizefight. Curley well knew Johnson hadn't fought since that significant afternoon in Reno in 1910, celebrated as the so-called Fight of the Century.

Curley had been deeply impressed by the job that promoter George "Tex" Rickard did to pull together Johnson's fight against Jim Jeffries two years before. At the last moment Rickard had been forced to move the bout from

San Francisco to Nevada, not an easy thing to manage. What is more, that contest brought in piles of money for everyone concerned. Though the Reno fray—a white man versus a black man—earned landmark status and drew a staggering crowd of twenty-two thousand, it nonetheless caused ugly pandemonium throughout the United States.

The promoter didn't believe that would happen again with Jack Johnson. Moreover, Curley was certain he could get another White Hope and pit him against Johnson. All Curley needed, he believed, was a "husky game fighter" who would gladly hop in the ring free of fright against the world's best heavyweight boxer. Whoever that white man might be, Curley thought, he had a good chance of making everyone as rich as Rockefeller.

While Curley was in Europe, he saw a great deal of Johnson. "He was much in evidence in the boulevard cafes," Curley said later. "Every time I saw him I felt as if some scrappy fellow would show up and take the title away from him."

When he returned to the United States, Curley looked at Carl Morris, the "Sapulpa Giant," and felt the big Oklahoman might be the best White Hope to take on Johnson.[2] Standing 6 feet, 4 inches, and weighing 240 pounds, Morris was an awesome sight.[3]

That idea ended when Jim Flynn, a fighter as mean as cat dirt, battered Morris into submission on September 15, 1911, in Madison Square Garden. Morris bled continually from the second round to the finish, as if an artery had been severed. In fact, the referee, who began the fight wearing a white shirt, found himself at the end dressed in crimson.

Before he traveled to New York, Flynn took off in mid-August for Lordsburg, New Mexico, where he coldcocked a stiff named George Haley, who was making his ring debut. Haley never fought again professionally.

A month later Flynn went to Oklahoma City where he flattened George Hess, another unknown. Those three maulings, not one of them terribly conclusive, nonetheless made Curley, an inveterate newspaper reader, sit up and think. It was just possible that Flynn, a Coloradoan with rough edges and truculent by nature, might well be his man. It did not seem to matter to Curley at all that, almost five years before, Johnson had handed Flynn such a beatdown in California that he had required serious medical attention.[4]

Some weeks after the Morris bout, Curley was seated in the Lambs Club in Chicago, in the company of Otto Floto, a Denver sporting editor. Two other gents of the press, Ed Smith of Chicago and Sandy Griswold of Omaha, also happened to be there. Curley brought up Flynn's name to the three journalists. It's not known if those writers had been drinking large amounts of alcohol. In any event, they agreed Flynn might well be the guy who could take down Johnson. In early October, Curley met with Flynn. The promoter wondered aloud what the Fireman, as he was called by many, thought of getting in the ring again with Johnson.

Flynn told Curley he had not challenged Johnson previously because he feared being roasted by the sporting writers and called a four-flusher.

In an effort to know the Fireman better, Curley took Flynn with him on a barnstorming wrestling tour. Flynn wasn't a wrestler. In fact, he scowled at the idea, but finally agreed to go along for the ride. At some point during that venture, Flynn confided to Curley these less-than-momentous words: "I know I can beat the big fellow."

Curley smiled. It was the sort of confidence that he wanted to hear. Though the wrestling expedition proved to be a financial flop, it did direct Curley's labors to laying a foundation for a heavyweight world championship prizefight. Moreover, it helped Curley set in motion a match with Johnson.

Not that Jack Johnson was a pushover. He could bob and weave as well as anyone. He could also punch. Fight fans know well the legendary tussle Johnson had with a middleweight, a tough-as-teak scrapper, named Stanley Ketchel. The undersized Ketchel sent Johnson to the floor in the twelfth round. Johnson quickly sprang to his feet and immediately decked Ketchel. A good hour passed before Ketchel stirred. Johnson had struck the "Michigan Assassin" with such ferocity that two of Ketchel's front teeth, torn from the gums, were found buried in Johnson's right glove.

On December 27, 1911, in Salt Lake City, Flynn gave Tony Caponi, a one-time coal miner, a belated Christmas present—a trip to the canvas in round two. No one considered Caponi a world-beater.[5] In fact, several people who attended that fight in Utah agreed that Flynn was a staunch and plucky hard hitter. Others in the crowd believed that Caponi took a dive.

Johnson was on his way back to America in the early autumn of 1911 and surely heard the news that Flynn might challenge him. Reporters in New York asked Johnson when he arrived in that city what it would take to be part of such a match.

"Thirty thousand dollars," said Johnson without pause. "Plus a thousand for expenses."

While other promoters dickered with Johnson, Curley stepped in. He went to Johnson's house in Chicago, where the champion was having a party. Johnson announced at the gathering that he had accepted Curley's offer, even though Curley had yet to make an offer. Johnson was excited over the prospect of a match with Flynn. The champion needed the money, for one. For two, he was certain that having shellacked Flynn once, a repeat would be as easy as shelling peas.

Just like that, Curley grabbed the match. Flynn at once proved his willingness to take a gamble so far as the financial part of the bout was concerned. He would be fighting for free, for nothing but a chance to become top of the heap.

The pairing was clinched verbally on New Year's Eve, and the preliminary articles signed a few days after in the parlor of Chicago's Hotel Sherman.

A portion of America got wind of the news in late December 1911. The fight was formally locked in on January 6. Contracts—then called Articles of Agreement—were signed in front of a phalanx of flashing cameras. Johnson was to receive $1,100 for training and traveling expenses. Win, lose, or draw, Johnson was guaranteed $31,000. He likely was amused at the mere notion of losing the fight, which would be held in July, with the date and place unclear.

Little in prizefighting is a sure thing.[6] A week after signing the articles, Johnson claimed that Flynn had gone back on his word and would challenge Al Palzer before July the Fourth. Doing so, Johnson said, would water down his match with Flynn. The Fireman must have guffawed. He then boasted, "I am not afraid of the champion and I believe that when he gets some of my holiday punches in his dinner bell he will feel his title slipping."

Perhaps to inflate Flynn's chances, Curley told the press that Johnson would be two years older since his last fight.[7] "The black man is thirty-five years of age or over, and has lived rapidly and never was a man-killer in the ring."

On January 18, Flynn showed he was up to the challenge of Johnson. He took on Al Williams in a match in Toronto and put the Californian to sleep in the tenth round. That would be Flynn's last appearance before his Fourth of July encounter.[8]

CHAPTER 2

The Minister of Propaganda

BY THE EARLY months of 1912, most Americans had learned of the Johnson-Flynn world heavyweight championship. A sizable number of newspaper readers knew that promoter Jack Curley had brought the two boxers together. What almost no one knew was the identity of the man who would soon begin to extol the upcoming championship as the most significant mano-a-mano showdown since little David pulled a stone from his sling and hurled a bull's-eye at Goliath in one swift toss.

Curley was positive he could drum up enough publicity to gull the public into believing Flynn had a chance. Johnson apparently agreed to go along with the plan. Fans nationwide were not interested in watching Johnson successfully defend his crown; they wanted only to see him laid to waste. Curley's publicity was based on this knowledge.

Two years before, Curley had witnessed the value of prefight hyperbole. James J. Corbett, who in 1892 had knocked out the great John L. Sullivan, sent out to the press a series of pronouncements outlining his vital role in monitoring the Jim Jefferies camp. Corbett, a crafty maneuverer known as Gentleman Jim, generated a good deal of press coverage by contrasting the heroic Jeffries with the dishonorable and generally inferior Johnson.

These news stories by Corbett were the beginnings of preprizefight exaggeration. Deep down Curley was sure this would be another Fight of the Century, a better one, in fact. This fight would, Curley was convinced, attract as much attention and as many spectators as Reno had for Johnson and Jeffries, if not more. To bolster such an eyebrow-raising intuition, Curley knew just the right person for the role, a man cut in the Jim Corbett mold of thumping the tubs.

That fellow is a largely forgotten member of the 1912 Flynn coterie.[1] And yet he had, with Curley's blessings, a self-imposed mission to singlehandedly spread the word about the event. This meant bloating interest in the pairing and hatching all sorts of contrivances to keep the sell going. As minister of propaganda, this man would send out absurd predictions, offer unrealistic opinions, inflate ticket sales, and boost attendance estimates.[2]

He would pass along to reporters how wonderful this athletic function would be. He created nonexistent tension, painted the site of the fight as a pristine castle in the sky, and made the entire affair far, far larger in importance than it had any right to be.

The publicist commissioned to take on these tasks was a dapper, Ivy League–educated newspaperman named Harold Webster Lanigan.[3] Most people called him Harry. To some he was Hal or even Lanny. Quite a few simply referred to him as Lanigan. His byline was H. W. Lanigan, but the majority of the news items that he puffed up about the looming fight and dispatched to various publications nationwide did not credit his name. Vain as he was, Lanigan made sure that plenty of reports did bear his byline.

Born in Brooklyn, New York, in 1875, Lanigan was the son of literary lights. His father, George T. Lanigan, a Canadian by birth, was a skilled journalist who had worked for the *Montreal Star*, the *New York World*, and finally the *Philadelphia Record*. He also composed poetry on the side. George Lanigan's wife, Bertha Spink Lanigan, was an early editor of the *Ladies Home Journal*.

George and Bertha produced two sports-writing sons, Harold and Ernest. Harold went off to the University of Pennsylvania, where he played rugby and baseball. Using his family credentials, Harold Lanigan acquired his first job as copyboy for the *Philadelphia Inquirer*. When their father died, the boys' mother sent the brothers to St. Louis to work for her brother, Alfred Spink, the editor of the *Sporting News*.

From there Harold moved to other St. Louis newspapers where he reported principally on baseball and boxing. A graceful writer, he could knock out stories as if his pants were on fire, some said.[4] When he left the *Sporting News*, Lanigan joined the *St. Louis Times*, for which he covered boxing under the credit line "Jab." At the same time Lanigan was writing about pugilism in St. Louis, Curley was arranging boxing cards in that city. The two men got to know each other.

Taken by Lanigan's journalism pedigree, his prizefight reportage, and his overall urbanity, Curley asked him to join the Flynn team as "press representative." The *Las Vegas Optic* would later describe Lanigan "as clever a sport writer as ever banged a typewriter with two fingers."

The well-togged Lanigan had left newspapering in 1911 to become the public-relations manager of a cushy resort in Hot Springs, Arkansas. His job was to flack the elegant Arlington Hotel, its popular mineral spa and casino, the Eastman Hotel, and the esteemed Oaklawn Park Race Track.

Hot Springs had long attracted well-heeled and big-name swells. Lanigan took the public relations role in Arkansas presumably because it paid more money than toiling in newspapering. He likely knew he was never going to be a shining star in journalism, certainly not like his brother Ernest, who became the premier professional baseball historian and statistician of the twentieth century. Ernest wrote the first baseball encyclopedia and was curator of the Baseball Hall of Fame in Cooperstown, New York, for two decades. His efforts related to the statistics side of baseball ultimately led to the creation of the Society for American Baseball Research, or SABR.

Jack Curley arrived in Hot Springs, Arkansas, on April 22, 1912, ostensibly to get Jim Flynn in shape for his meet-up with Johnson. Flynn loved to play the ponies. In fact, he seemed to spend more time at Oaklawn than he did in a gym.

"Flynn is here for a brief course of the baths and well-earned rest," the Hot Springs newspaper observed. What made it "well-earned" was perplexing. Flynn had not fought since September 1911 and in the interim he had gone on a fourteen-week tour as a vaudeville act, mostly talking about his life, much as Johnson did.

Curley, now reunited with Lanigan in Hot Springs, was joined there by Arthur Greiner, a to-the-manor-born Chicago crony of Curley's. Greiner, the high-living son of a Chicago leather-goods king, drove racing cars, though not for a living because he did not need to work. The press liked to refer to socialites Curley and Greiner as "men about town."[5]

The *Hot Springs Sentinel-Record* referred to Greiner as "a famous athlete." Greiner would assist in the conditioning of Flynn. Exactly how that would be achieved was never quite explained. Greiner's brief career as an athlete was largely spent parked on an automobile seat. If a boxer finds himself seated on the canvas, it's a sure sign something has gone terribly wrong. Early fame came to Greiner in 1910 when race-car drivers stood out as being physically reckless. Greiner's foolhardiness seemed to know no bounds.

Lanigan jumped at the chance to become part of something that, if Flynn won, might lead those accompanying the challenger to fame and recognition, not to mention wealth. Lanigan's job description, if it existed, was to gin up the Fourth of July fight using every possible means. He would also shoulder other matters that Curley might find for him.

Lanigan went to work immediately in Hot Springs. He forwarded to dozens of newspapers a blizzard of stories and photographs of Flynn training, or pretending to train. Lanigan directed a hired local photographer to capture Flynn taking a "mild drill" over the hills during his first afternoon there. Mild drill? That meant no more than a casual hike.

After that training ramble, Flynn climbed into a mineral bath, received a rubdown, and then stepped on a scale. He weighed 216 pounds. How much Flynn and Johnson weighed were figures that, thanks in large part to Hal Lanigan, spawned nationwide interest daily, right up until the opening gong of the fight.

Curley, Flynn, Lanigan, and Greiner spent more than a week in Arkansas—at the racetrack or in the Arlington Hotel—planning strategy and living the good life. So much of the bout's success would depend on getting the word out—and then, if need be, embellishing and overstating that word. At the same time, H. W. Lanigan would be telling readers the magnitude of this contest, how legitimate it was going to be, and how skilled the two pugilists were.

Nearly every day Lanigan churned out stories that detailed how Flynn was rounding into marvelous shape. How Curley was managing things so very well. How half of the country would be on hand for the "big battle," as the fight was now called by Lanigan and soon by sporting writers everywhere.

The upcoming event, Curley believed, would help earn him the stature of another Tex Rickard. Curley told a Hot Springs reporter that the fight between Flynn and Johnson would take in $100,000. Only the 1910 Johnson-Jeffries receipts would eclipse what Curley envisioned. The Fourth of July fight would be Flynn's greatest chance at the most coveted crown in sport.

Before Curley and company left Arkansas, two unsettling incidents occurred. On April 26, Curley received a telegram from the assistant sporting editor of the *Chicago Examiner*.[6] Jack Johnson had been in an automobile accident near Pittsburgh, the message said. Johnson had suffered a wrenched back, but that was not going to halt his match. According to the telegram, there was "absolutely nothing to worry about."

"Jack Johnson was not badly hurt," the *Hot Springs Sentinel-Record* wrote. The Associated Press, however, put on the wire what later turned out to be untrue. That was a story that Johnson had been seriously injured. Upon learning of that account, a deep gulp from Curley could almost be heard nationwide.

During the group's stay in Hot Springs, Curley set up an exhibition for Flynn in Wichita, Kansas, to be held on May 3 in that city's Forum. Tickets would go on sale a week before the scheduled event.

The Flynn contingent, which included a trainer, several sparring mates, and wrestlers, left Chicago by train and arrived in Wichita on the second day in May. The exhibition would feature Flynn going four rounds with Al Williams, now the Fireman's top stable hand.

Moments before the exhibition began, the manager of the Forum was notified that it was against the law to hold boxing exhibitions of any kind where tickets were sold.[7] Flynn went on stage anyway. He skipped rope a bit and briefly did some "imitation fighting" with Williams. Instead of an exhibition prizefight, several men with the Flynn assemblage wrestled, including Williams, who was a boxer. One of the wrestling matches was stopped by the Wichita police.

The entire affair proved to be a disaster. It would foreshadow the often sloppy two-plus months that lay ahead. Indeed, Wichita was the beginning of numerous blunders by Curley, who went along with the Flynn camp on the 1400-mile round-trip journey to Kansas. More importantly, Curley had not inquired prior to that train ride whether professional boxing in the Kansas community was legal.

That failure emphasized Curley's inability to stay on track, as well as his slapdash manner of putting together matters of significance. Undaunted by the Wichita bungle, Curley gathered the Flynn congregation and headed for Colorado, Jim Flynn's home state, his provenance. There, led by H. W. Lanigan's inexhaustible labors, the publicity wheels began to turn rapidly and outlandishly.

CHAPTER 3

Home Sweet Hype

WHILE JACK JOHNSON did his training for the fight at Bill McConnell's gymnasium in Chicago—and according to many sources, he did so only when he felt the urge—Jim Flynn & Company was on the move. Flynn, Curley, Arthur Greiner, H. W. Lanigan, and sparring partner Al Williams arrived in Denver on May 6, 1912, the first stop on a swing through Colorado.

Flynn boxed four rounds that night at Denver's Baker Theater. He received a rousing ovation from a jam-packed house when he walked out on the stage. The Fireman quickly displayed a rarely heard sense of humor. "I am confident I am going to win on July the Fourth," Flynn told the audience. "There is no chance of me colliding with any icebergs or a black man's fist."[1]

Then Flynn said something nice about his opponent, also unusual for him. "I want Johnson at his best and am glad to know that he was not hurt in that automobile spill in Pittsburgh."

A week later found Johnson jogging over Chicago's South Side boulevards and starting in on some ring work. The *Chicago Daily Tribune*'s Walter Eckersall wrote that Johnson had hurt his shoulder but was much better.

"With proper treatment, my shoulder will mend quickly," Johnson told Eckersall. Then the champion added, "Unless I have underrated Flynn, I should stop him inside of ten rounds."

If such words got back to Flynn, they surely must have galled him and his troupe.

On May 7, the Flynn bunch was off to Colorado Springs, where they stayed at the Antlers Hotel and where the challenger talked to the press.[2] "I am going to surprise some of the wise ones on Independence Day," Flynn said.

A scale at the Antlers showed Flynn weighed 211 pounds. Curley told onlookers Flynn would enter the ring at 188 pounds, but likely 198.

"Flynn is in the pink of condition," the *Colorado Springs Gazette* reported. "He is taking care of himself and who knows, he may be a true prophet."

Prophet or not, Flynn seemed to struggle with facts this day. He said he was not the same man whom Johnson knocked out in eleven rounds back in 1907. "Nor is Jack in the same shape now as then. Then I was a comparatively green fighter." (Truth: he'd already had more than fifty bouts.) "Why, I only weighed 158 pounds in 1907." (Truth: he weighed 174 pounds.) "Johnson was in his prime, between the ages of twenty-nine and thirty-two. I think Johnson now is thirty-seven years old." (Truth: he was thirty-four years old.)

The omnipresent H. W. Lanigan, perhaps made uneasy by Flynn's statements, took over the press conference. "When the match was first proposed," Lanigan said, "it was met with ridicule. Now Flynn is gaining new backers every day. The fight fans are warming up to Jim and they are all for him to win."

The Flynn team left Colorado Springs at eleven o'clock the next morning and arrived in Pueblo at noon on May 8. The purpose behind stopping at these places was clearly to plug the fight mightily. And no place was more important to call upon than Pueblo, Colorado, Flynn's adopted hometown. Though he was born in Hoboken, New Jersey, Flynn grew up in Pueblo. That was where he had many friends, as well as kin, and where lacing on boxing gloves drew his initial and immediate interest.

One of the first fights Flynn had does not appear in any record books.[3] It took place in the main dining room of Pueblo's St. James Hotel, most likely in the 1890s. The fight was part of a show put on by Bat Masterson, he of pistol-packing lawman fame, and Otto Floto of *Denver Post* sports-writing acclaim. Flynn's opponent that night was Mexican Pete Everett, an unschooled plodder.

It's a little-known fact that Jack Johnson, in the very early years of the last century, briefly relocated to western Colorado, to the mining camps of Cripple Creek and Victor, in search of matches. Flynn drifted there too, for the same reason. Both left there with easy wins. There is no record that their paths crossed in the Rockies.

On that night in the St. James Hotel, Masterson reportedly presented Flynn with a badge that said "Sheriff of Tombstone." Supposedly Flynn then asked Masterson, "How many men did you kill at the OK Corral?"[4]

Coincidentally, Masterson would soon wind up in New York City as the sporting editor of the *Morning Telegraph*. Not surprisingly, the chief character in the Runyon's grandest theatrical production was "Sky" Masterson.

Those were colorful days in Pueblo. The soon-to-be esteemed Damon Runyon, who was born in Kansas, had recently begun a career as a newspaper reporter in Pueblo. That chosen line of work led him to New York City where he wrote a well-read newspaper column. There Runyan gave fellow Coloradoan Jack Dempsey the colorful nickname "the Manassa Mauler." If that wasn't enough, Runyan created the wildly popular Broadway musical *Guys and Dolls*.

In time Runyan befriended Jack Johnson. Of that event, Runyan wrote: "I saw Jack's limousine blocking traffic in the Paris boulevards while the white people struggled to shake hands with the burly black man."[5]

As much as Flynn cared for Pueblo, some residents of that city supposedly held a secret about him. Twenty years after Flynn's 1912 fight with Johnson, Jack Curley penned a malicious article in *The Ring* magazine that painted Flynn as a crude reprobate. Curley wrote, "Flynn had not been back home since the day he beat up the chief of police and two policemen and made his escape on a switch engine he found in the station. The police apparently forgot the incident or forgave him."

If Curley's memory was accurate, all was now forgiven. When Flynn stepped off the train at Pueblo's Union Station this May morning in 1912, he was met by a brass band that immediately broke into—to no one's surprise—"All Coons Look Alike to Me." The song was scheduled to be heard at the Jeffries fight, but canceled because of racial fears. It would more than likely be heard again in Las Vegas.

Hundreds of fans hailed Flynn's presence and a parade soon formed along Main Street.[6] Cars honked and spectators cheered as the procession made its way through Pueblo's business district. Eight people sat in the lead car, an open-top roadster. Among the passengers were Curley; Al Williams, Flynn's sparring partner; Lanigan; and the driver, Henry Rhubesky of Pueblo. The mayor of Pueblo—T. D. Donnelly—and Arthur Greiner also squeezed into a seat.

Making sure he was seen, Flynn stood up in the huge car as it slowly moved along. To the surge of people lining the street he waved and broke into a crooked smile. When Flynn spotted his mother, Mrs. Hector Chiariglione, also known as Mayme, he blew her a kiss.

That evening, when Flynn walked across the stage at Pueblo's Pantages Theater, a bouquet of roses greeted him as did another round of applause.[7] He sparred four rounds with Al Williams that night. The *Pueblo Star-Journal* reported the theater to be filled with fans who "cheered the big Fireman lustily and shouted their approbation when he made a chopping block out of Williams."

Flynn's entire education had been in Pueblo. Though he gave the impression of being something of an uncouth lout, especially later in his career, Flynn stood out at Pueblo's Centennial High School.[8] He was a star athlete at the school, he ran track, and he played catcher and the infield for the school's baseball team.

As a member of the Bulldogs football squad, Flynn lined up as a receiver. During that May 1912 visit, Pueblo's *Star-Journal* newspaper mentioned that Flynn "did not complete his course of study." Yet school records today show he graduated from Centennial with the class of 1899.

Flynn was, wrote *Star-Journal* reporter Harold Zeiger, willing to debate Johnson, who had but a fifth-grade education, on any topic the champion might choose. At Centennial High, Flynn had been a member of the Pnyx Debating Society.

"If the fight on July the Fourth was to be in logic instead of with gloves, the odds would favor Flynn," Zeiger wrote. Flynn was apparently remembered in Pueblo as being able to put up a pretty good argument with almost anyone.

Flynn's prowess with his fists earned the respect of his Pueblo schoolmates. He was often pitted against the best athletes on other schools' sports teams. A speedy runner, he supposedly was able to race one hundred yards in ten seconds.

Flynn's most steadfast admirer was Charles Patrick, the sporting editor of the *Pueblo Star-Journal*. During Flynn's stay in Pueblo, Patrick wrote that Johnson shirked training. "So far Johnson has not arranged his training camp or gone into active training. The difference between the two fighters is worth noting and unless the colored champion gets to work in a short time, he will not be the man he was when he met Jeffries. He needs training more than Flynn and if he doesn't get into first-class condition he will surely surrender the title when he meets the Puebloan on July Fourth."

During Flynn's sparring session at the Pantages, the fighter's physique left Patrick nearly breathless. "Jim's shoulders and back development are wonderful," Patrick enthused. "His arms are tremendous and he has developed the short, choppy blows which he has made famous in the ring to such an extent that every time he landed on Williams last night, he made Williams wince with pain."

Patrick's praise for the local star knew no end. "Jim's footwork is marvelous. He is as fast as a bantam on his feet and his guard is almost impenetrable. Williams never touched him with a glove in the four rounds of fighting."

More and more Patrick laid on the flattery, thick as a brick. Indeed, some readers must have thought by the sporting editor's words that the world championship had already been decided.

"In defensive work Flynn has improved wonderfully," Patrick noted. "He never leaves himself open and is always set for one of those terrific short-arm blows, which he has. If the Negro champion accepts this style of clashing during the battle, he will find himself in great distress and danger."

A banquet and reception at Pueblo's Hotel Vail, which was open to the public, came after the sparring. Mayor Donnelly told those present that Flynn was "the greatest Pueblo booster." Flynn, the mayor went on, "gave the city much good exposure."

The public display of affection for Flynn seemed unceasing. Otto Floto, the *Denver Post* sporting editor, delivered an over-the-top tribute to Flynn. "I want to tell you that this Pueblo boy is the greatest fighter in the world today. Those who are figuring an easy victory for Johnson will have another thing coming. I don't figure but one result: a victory for Flynn."

Finally, Jack Curley stood up and continued with this love fest. "I, of course, feel that Flynn is going to win this fight," Curley proclaimed. "He is the greatest fighting machine in the world today and has developed a style of defense and attack that will be all new to Johnson. He will simply walk into the ring and worry Johnson to death."

To this Curley added, "For all Flynn's triumphs in the fight game, the Puebloan is still a locomotive fireman." (Truth: Flynn had not picked up a coal shovel in several years.)

Eventually, Flynn got a chance to speak at the banquet. He did not mince words. "I am going to knock the Negro stiff. I am going to bring back the championship where it belongs: to a white man. I promise that I will win and after July the Fourth, the championship flag will be flying over this old town."

The applause that followed was earsplitting.

Early the next day Flynn took the bouquet he had been given and, accompanied by Al Williams, went to Flynn's mother's cottage in Bessemer, a blue-collar neighborhood that sat among Pueblo's familiar steel mills. Flynn had purchased the house on Broadway Street for his mother with the percentage of the money he earned when he fought Sam Langford in 1908.

Langford had won that fight on a knockout. But in Bessemer this day, no one cared. Putting that loss aside, Flynn and Williams sat down with Flynn's relatives to a home-cooked meal.

Meanwhile, H. W. Lanigan was cooking up something of his own. On May 9, Flynn was appointed chief editor of the *Pueblo Star-Journal's* sports page. Only Lanigan could have devised such a gimmicky idea. There would be articles on that page contributed by Flynn, Curley, Al Williams, and even Flynn's mother. All of these stories and even some in Pueblo's other daily newspaper, the *Chieftain*, would be authored by Lanigan.

According to the *Star-Journal*, "Jim will tell his own story of the Johnson fight and just how he expected to beat the colored champion and bring home to Pueblo the championship."

In a Lanigan-concocted piece of journalism that bore a Jim Flynn byline in the *Chieftain*, Flynn "wrote" the following: "While I have been taking care of myself, building up like I never have heard of a man taking on weight and strength without getting fat, what has our friend been doing? I'll tell you, although I hate to say anything against Johnson. He has been stepping over champagne corks at a rate that would put the average man in the down-and-out club in a hurry.

"He cannot stand this and it is sure to tell on him. If the fight goes twelve rounds, I will win."[9]

Flynn, using Lanigan's script, didn't stop there. "Now I have a defense that is a dandy. I won't go into this bout and get an eye closed with the first crack of the bat, as I did the last time with Johnson [their 1907 fight]. I can beat any man in the world at infighting."

Speaking for himself, the tireless Lanigan wrote that he had known Curley for fifteen years but Flynn for barely a month. "I can truthfully state," Lanigan proclaimed, "that Jim is all man." (Those words surely brought newspaper readers a sigh of relief). Lanigan went on to tell Coloradoans that Flynn had made a big hit at Hot Springs and was much in demand before he left. "At dances at the Arlington Hotel Jim was always popular and people were sorry to see him leave. He is a gentleman who does not drink or smoke or chew." (Truth: he preferred a lager and a hand-rolled Bull Durham.)

Lanigan could write like a whiz, but fact-checking was not his forte. He outdid himself by crafting a two-hundred-word, first-person testimonial, allegedly composed by Flynn's mom.

The press agent put theses sentences into the woman's mouth: "I have every reason to believe Jim is the best man in the world and I will not be a bit worried over the outcome. I have not the slightest idea but that he will return from Las Vegas the world's undisputed champion. He has always been a winner since he was a little boy."[10] (Truth: Flynn had lost sixteen professional fights before his July date with Johnson.) "He just kept working all the time with the plan of becoming the greatest boxer in the world. And I think he has just about arrived at his goal."

She, or rather Lanigan, was not quite through sharing this information. "I guess there were some tough ones in the fight game and it is not the most attractive life. But Jim is a good boy and I am proud of him."

Flynn's every move in Pueblo, his every remark, produced a reaction. When he arrived by train in Pueblo, Flynn had $8,000 in his pocket. He went straight to the First National Bank in Pueblo where he deposited $7,500 of it.[11] After his 1911 bout with Carl Morris at Madison Garden in New York City, Flynn placed a check for $6,000 in that same Pueblo bank.

"Flynn believes in Pueblo dollars for Pueblo men," a May 9 article in the *Pueblo Chieftain* pointed out with deep pride. "Jim believes in keeping his money at home." The article said that the Fireman owned a farm, some real estate, lots of bonds, some good stocks, and a bank account "that was piling up rapidly."

Writing under Jack Curley's name, Lanigan went for the heartstrings: "To Pueblo, Flynn will remain plain Jim Flynn, the Fighting Fireman. Win or lose, he will be welcomed home as the man who performed earnestly, willingly and honestly."

That was followed by this whopper: "Even if the whole world, including the citizens of Pueblo, turn their backs upon him, should he prove the loser, the outstretched arms of a mother's love will be waiting at 323 Broadway Street to welcome home her boy."

Before that welcoming could happen, a site for the Johnson-Flynn fight had to be chosen.

CHAPTER 4

Which Way to South Porcupine?

WITH THE I's dotted, the t's crossed, and the contracts signed, Jack Curley began looking over prospective sites for the fight's location.[1] California was rejected due to the 1910 last-minute switch from San Francisco to Reno for the Johnson-Jeffries fight and the trouble that had caused.

New Orleans was also nixed because that city barred fights between black and white boxers. Great Britain did not make the cut, nor did Australia. New York City was quickly dropped from the running. Why? Curley knew there was no love lost between Johnson and the New York Boxing Commission.

Curley took a shine to towns that sat along the Western Pacific Railroad. He met with railroad officials, but nothing panned out. Meanwhile, numerous metropolises, including a handful of tiny homesteads named Metropolis, expressed an interest in holding the fight. These communities ranged widely, from the unsurprising to the unconventional.

Take South Porcupine, Ontario, for instance. It stood east of Lake Superior but close to the Canadian city of Timmins. A town named South Porcupine surely must have generated some amusement.

Did anyone actually live there?[2] It is likely that few were taking South Porcupine seriously until it was learned that a gold rush had gone on in South Porcupine and in Porcupine proper from 1909 to 1911. There was still gold in mines there, according to Casey Moran, who edited the *Mining Investor* newspaper. That said, Moran was ready to put forth $50,000 to gain the fight.[3]

A group of sporting men in Bassano, Canada, also was willing to share the limelight with the same amount to secure a spot in prizefight lore. Politicians in Nevada and Utah showed interest, as did officials in Juarez, Mexico, and neighboring El Paso, Texas. A syndicate of wealthy oil operators offered stacks of money to bring the fight to Casper, Wyoming. City fathers in Albuquerque and Santa Fe also displayed an eagerness to be involved in the decision.

There were only two places on a map of the world where Curley initially hoped to win the fight—Paris and one of the hustling towns in the Canadian Northwest, such as Bassano, which was "bidding recklessly for the championship," the *Sporting News* reported.

Out of nowhere came a good faith overture from some New Mexico businessmen. It was accompanied by $1,000 in cash, for expenses. Curley swiftly went to Las Vegas to meet with Charles O'Malley, who was the guest of honor at a dinner there. The promoter shook hands with O'Malley and then did likewise with William McDonald, the governor of New Mexico. McDonald told Curley he hoped the promoter would bring the fight to Las Vegas. "If you do, you may count upon any aid I can give you."[4]

Those words would ultimately turn as empty as a discarded shoe. Curley found the enthusiasm in Las Vegas so pronounced and the governor so cordial that the promoter was ready to commit on the spot.

When newspapers said Las Vegas, New Mexico, had entered the conversation, the idea was met mostly with bewilderment. To a reasonable portion of the United States, that city and state were not geographically well known. In fact, many newspaper readers thought New Mexico still belonged to Mexico. Not everyone was happy with Las Vegas's intention to put on the fight. Indeed, the *Albuquerque Morning Journal* accused the *Las Vegas Optic* of zealous boosterism by advertising the community in the most advantageous ways. Clearly jealousy was behind such an opinion.[5]

News of a bid of $100,000 for the fight swiftly arrived in New Mexico.[6] Much of that sum was helped by the Las Vegas Athletic Club. Not surprisingly, the figure made headlines. In the gaining of statehood, no law in New Mexico prohibited such contests and no ceiling on the cost of this prizefight existed.

The prodigious amount from New Mexico was not immediately accepted, which even now seems difficult to fathom. Curley simply seemed hesitant. He said he had to study proposals from Albuquerque and Santa Fe, among other cities.

A more likely explanation for the delay by Curley arrived early in February. Curley, it was learned, had gone to San Francisco to talk with James

Coffroth, a nationally known and greatly experienced prizefight promoter. Curley asked Coffroth to assist him with managing the New Mexico bout. New to the prizefight game, Curley surely needed help. For whatever reason, Coffroth declined to lend him a hand. That rejection would prove significant in the weeks ahead and on through to the fight itself. Simply, one incongruous incident after another seemed to emanate from Las Vegas.[7]

On April 18, Curley, who by now had become Flynn's manager, traveled to New Mexico with Art Greiner, a close buddy from Chicago days. The *Albuquerque Morning Journal* caught up with the two sporting men at the railroad station. The Chicago pals were on their way to Las Vegas, the newspaper learned, to investigate the city as a possible venue for the fight.

Greiner's specific task would be to look over the famed Montezuma Hotel, with its nearby hot springs, and to see about reopening the hotel. For several years the Montezuma was the crown jewel of the Santa Fe Railroad system.[8] However, the Montezuma had suffered two fires since its construction in 1879 as a luxury inn. It had been shuttered for some time. There had been rumors that the hotel's owners were to get the Montezuma back on its feet and return it to one of the country's great resorts, a hostelry that catered especially to the moneybags of sporting men and tourists. A horse-racing track was also being considered for the Montezuma, Curley had heard, a venue to rival the well-known Don Alberto Terrazas Park in Ciudad Juarez. It would take more than a million dollars to do this, but hopes were high it would happen.

Upon reaching Las Vegas, Greiner made a close inspection of the Montezuma, a stunning castle-like edifice that sat at the mouth of Gallinas Canyon. The hotel's adjacent warm springs made it doubly attractive, for its waters were said to decisively treat an assortment of bodily aches and pains.

The hotel had been the first place in the area to have electric lights. The two fires—in 1880 and 1885—caused severe damage to the structure, and in 1903 the Montezuma closed. The hotel's casino, untouched by the flames, was habitable. In fact, Curley saw it as an acceptable training center for Flynn and his sparring mates. The Flynn gang would eat and sleep in the hotel caretaker's cottage, which was close by. Curley and Greiner would stay in a downtown Las Vegas hotel.

Art Greiner, Curley was certain, would somehow persuade the powers at be to return the Montezuma to its glorious beginnings. Because so many thousands of visitors were expected at the fight in New Mexico, Las Vegas needed to have numerous places to stay. La Castaneda, the pride of the Harvey House chain, would be used, of course, as would the Plaza Hotel. However, the Plaza wouldn't reopen until late in June after undergoing some repairs. That left many people wondering this: "Where is everybody going to stay?"

As an amateur race-car driver, Greiner had been successful. However, as a professional in the first Indianapolis 500 race, on May 30, 1911, Greiner finished dead last. Now he had failed once more. He could not induce the Montezuma's titleholder to unlock its doors. In fact, never again would the majestic edifice serve as a hotel.

If Curley was upset, he did not express it. Greiner, after all, was a good friend. And Curley, who was already being slammed in the press for putting his faith in what looked by many to be a one-sided bout, needed all the friends he could get.

Curley had invited Greiner to join him in New Mexico likely because Greiner had been criticized widely at that initial Indianapolis race. The press came down hard on Greiner for his insistence on getting into a race car that exhibited a wobbly right rear wheel. Greiner in fact had been warned about this problem. Ignoring the warnings, Greiner crashed on lap number one.[9]

Indy cars then had open cockpits and no windshields. Tragically, the accident claimed the life of Greiner's mechanic, Sam Dickson, who was riding with Greiner, a common occurrence at that time. Dickson was propelled upward from the vehicle and then slammed headfirst into the earth. His body was reported to be "badly mangled." Greiner, too, had been launched from the cockpit. He suffered a broken arm but otherwise survived the horrific accident.

Even without the Montezuma, three Las Vegas businessmen managed to bring the fight to New Mexico. As their leader, Charles Francis O'Malley, nicknamed "King," had a monarchial bearing. Each year, atop a white stallion, he led the Rough Riders reunion parade. To numerous townspeople, O'Malley seemed the perfect choice to help bring such an important event to their doorstep. For one, he was an excellent and well-respected entrepreneur who grew up in Louisiana and then pulled himself up by his bootstraps in the wide-open West.

Moreover, everyone knew O'Malley was immensely fond of sports. In fact, it was said that he had participated in athletics at the very highest level.[10]

According to Las Vegas belief, O'Malley had played baseball as a pitcher for either the St. Louis Cardinals or the St. Louis Browns, or perhaps both.[11] O'Malley's relatives and friends were sure he had suited up for the Cardinals from 1896 to 1899. It's possible he may have pitched some batting practices way back when, but that is like someone saying they ran a marathon when in truth they dropped out after two miles.

In any case, facts cannot be altered. *The Baseball Encyclopedia*, the game's official record book, indicates that Charles F. O'Malley never competed in major-league baseball. A reliable online minor-league directory shows no Charles O'Malley on its rolls either. Supposedly, O'Malley had boxed as a young man while serving in the Navy. Information about his bouts was unavailable.

O'Malley, it was often repeated, had served as a freelance scout for the Browns at the turn of the century. It's quite possible that he may have done that part-time. If so, baseball scouting appeared to be the extent of his actual athletic achievements.

All of this, of course, brings forth a questionable sports accomplishment of another New Mexican, also a pitcher. Former governor Bill Richardson steadfastly believed he had been drafted by a major-league baseball team, although he eventually admitted he had not.

Annie Leonard, who is O'Malley's great-granddaughter, was not surprised to learn recently that O'Malley did not participate in one inning in the big leagues. Leonard is fifty-four years old and lives in Knoxville, Iowa. Grandpa O'Malley, which Leonard had always called him, "never talked about it." In other words, if he did play professional baseball, he likely would have told stories about those days.

In dozens of 1912 newspaper articles, when the fight was announced, and much later in two books, O'Malley's baseball credentials were proudly accepted. The O'Malley family, it seemed, took the baseball background for granted and never challenged it. Nor did townspeople in Las Vegas. They knew Charles O'Malley as a superb businessman, a hard worker, a prominent citizen, a civic leader, and the longtime chief of the East Las Vegas Fire Department.

At some point, O'Malley apparently decided that baseball was once a part of his life. When O'Malley arrived in Las Vegas in 1900, a newcomer who knew not a soul, he yearned for the town's approval. If truth be known, he really didn't need respect.

Joining O'Malley in bargaining for the prizefight were the mayor of Las Vegas, Robert Taupert, who owned a jewelry store and watch-repair enterprise, and Ed Plowman, who supervised La Castaneda Hotel, a showpiece in the chain of Harvey Houses that stood along railroad stations in the western United States. Taupert and Plowman were looked up to in the community, though neither of the two had anything close to the alleged professional sports connections of "King" O'Malley.

Las Vegas did not possess a lot of name recognition in 1912, but it clearly had a good deal of history. Founded in 1835, Las Vegas had been a cow town, a sheep town, a railroad town, and a college town. Members of the earliest pueblos journeyed to the thermal springs in the area as long ago as AD 800.

By 1912, Las Vegas was a far cry from being a hardscrabble village, such as the various rough-and-tumble mining camps that somehow found a way into a discussion of the fight. How any of those locales made it onto Curley's list of potential site choices is anyone's guess. After all, much of the world would be aware of this prizefight. It wasn't going to be held in some Podunk barroom.

More than a century ago, Las Vegas was a bustling destination and had been since the railroad arrived. With a population of more than nine thousand in 1912, Las Vegas was the third largest city in New Mexico.[12]

By the time 1912 came around, Las Vegas was home to twelve churches, ten schools, four banks, and twenty-three fraternal organizations. Six newspapers were published there, including one daily. A handsome Carnegie Public Library that cost $20,000 graced the town. Also there were four sanitariums, an opera house, a railway hospital, two ice plants, and an insane asylum. Las Vegas was a wool center and a stock-raising hub. At 6,470 feet above sea level, the city stood where the Sangre de Cristo Mountains met the Staked Plains, otherwise known as the Llano Estacado.

With more than a dozen saloons in operation, Las Vegas definitely had some rough roots. The city's mostly sunny climate attracted numerous tuberculars, as well as those with bronchial and malarial troubles, brain fag, scrofula, catarrh, dropsy, and a slew of other maladies that are long past being footnotes in medical textbooks.

If there was one overriding disorder in Las Vegas, it was a general breakdown from overwork. Residents in 1912 were definitely not lazy.

For decades, Las Vegas was actually two communities, East Las Vegas and

West Las Vegas. A plaza anchored the west side of the community while Midwest-style buildings and a proper town square gave focus to the east side.

The seat of San Miguel County, Las Vegas in 1912 was not at all a wholesome city. People who passed through openly carried guns in the streets and had done so for many years.

While the railroad brought Las Vegas prosperity, the city likewise became a magnet for a wide range of citizens. Professional businessmen as well as schoolteachers, church folk, and cowboys could be found there. By the same token, so could murderers, swindlers, gamblers, and tramps. Dance-hall girls and prostitutes, thieves, rustlers, vigilantes, and an army of ornery characters such as Kickapoo George, Hog-Foot Jim, Cock-Eyed Frank, and so forth made their way through in the early days of the town's existence.[13]

The most vicious outlaw and the nastiest gang in Las Vegas was Vicente Silva and his Forty Thieves. Nothing stopped Silva or his henchmen. Silva kidnapped his own daughter for ransom, killed his wife for her money, and ordered her body be thrown into an arroyo. He murdered his brother-in-law and had his body tossed into the pit of an outhouse. A member of his gang eventually knocked off Silva by firing a bullet into his left temple.

At one time or another, celebrated folk of every stripe resided in Las Vegas. Doc Holliday, the consumptive dentist, was said to be a gunfighter when he wasn't yanking teeth or running a saloon on Centre Street. For a while, Wyatt Earp and his brother James Earp joined Holliday in Las Vegas in the running of a gambling enterprise.

Jesse James and Billy the Kid supposedly spent a few days and perhaps nights in the Montezuma Hotel, though not together. The two men were there to look things over. Kit Carson, it was believed, hung out for a spell in what became known as the Meadow City for its hushed grasslands and endless prairie.

Perhaps the biggest allure in the territorial frontier of Las Vegas was the hanging windmill that stood in the center of the plaza. In 1861, a feisty woman named Paula Angel, also known as Pablita Martin and Pablita Sandoval, was found guilty by a jury of murdering Juan Miguel Martin, said to be her lover.[14] Angel's age was somewhere between nineteen and twenty-six.

Judge Kirby Benedict, a nasty drunk who held his job only because of his friendship with Abraham Lincoln, sentenced Angel to be hanged until dead on April 26. Benedict also ordered Angel to pay the costs of services that would be involved in her upcoming execution. It was said that Benedict taunted her often during the days leading up to the hanging.

Paula Angel did not get hanged from the plaza's windmill but from a cottonwood tree in a grove on the northwest edge of town. Nonetheless, a large crowd showed up to watch. Angel had the distinction of being hanged not once but twice. The first time, a noose was slipped around her neck, but the sheriff forgot to bind her hands.

When the wagon she stood on was sent forward, Angel used her hands to grab the noose above her and then attempted to pull herself up. The sheriff rushed over and tied her hands. This time the hanging didn't fail.

Las Vegas grew and prospered with the railroad. Yet at the same time, good ideas there had a way of turning bad.[15] The ghastly hanging of Paula Angel is clearly one of several blunders.

In those young days of Las Vegas, an energetic, forward-thinking gent named Jose Albino Baca directed the construction of a mammoth, four-story building near the Santa Fe Railroad depot. The structure was erected to greet newcomers who were disembarking by rail. But passengers rarely stayed at the Baca mansion. In a short time, the great structure became a white elephant, a vacant laughingstock known as "Baca's Folly."[16]

In 1903, Las Vegas opened a territorial fair that promoters believed would surpass the Albuquerque territorial fair. That did not happen. A flood washed away the grandstand and ruined the racetrack. The fair reopened in 1905, to success, but then closed for good. It was believed that the shutting down of the electric trolley in the city was the cause.

During the dawn of the 1900s, a scenic road in Las Vegas was begun. It would lead sightseers into the Gallinas Canyon, which offered visitors stunning vistas. A large delegation from Las Vegas traveled to Santa Fe to obtain convict laborers to construct the road. A highline was built up along the cliffs of the canyon, and an exaggerating brochure was published. The brochure featured glowing words that could have come from H. W. Lanigan, the press agent for the Johnson-Flynn bout: "The beauties that this road will bring are in easy reach of all." Alas, those beauties turned out to be out of reach and the road was never completed.

The stigma of only partial accomplishment seemed to accompany all activities in Las Vegas. Through those raw years the town cultivated many events only to see those events fizzle. A cowboy reunion folded for lack of money. As did a horse show, motorboat races on nearby Storrie Lake, a polo club, and an ice-skating carnival on the Gallinas ice dam.

In the summer of 1899, Colonel Theodore Roosevelt arrived in town amid much fanfare to attend the first gathering of his famed Rough Riders. The annual reuniting did well for several years. However, as had so many other good ideas, this one eventually disappeared. The deaths of elderly Rough Riders through the years can only partially explain its demise. A lack of finances during the Depression must receive most of the blame.

By 1905, railroad traffic, and stature as the principal commercial center, began to wane more than ever in Las Vegas. City fathers looked for other ways of boosting the community. Hopeful signs appeared in Las Vegas during the first two decades of the twentieth century. Tom Mix, the cowboy actor, and auteur filmmaker Romaine Fielding often made short films in and around Las Vegas. That brush with fame did not last long, however. Mix and Fielding found better locations closer to Hollywood. Regrettably, many of the Las Vegas films that came out during that time were lost.

As if to add injury to insult, M. J. Brown, a journalist from Bryan, Ohio, visited Las Vegas in 1910 and published a spiteful report in the Bryan Democrat, a semiweekly newspaper.[7] The result made the New Mexico community appear to be a dystopian landscape.

"People come here to try dry farming," Brown wrote. "The sun beats down three hundred days of the year and people soon leave by prairie schooner." Brown arrived in Las Vegas by train. He had picked the town because he wanted to get away from Harvey House meals for twenty-four hours.

In his brief time in Las Vegas, Brown was dismayed to learn about the Penitentes, or Mexican self-scourgers, who lived nearby. "During the forty days of Lent," Brown wrote, "these people turn into "half-crazy fanatics." He found that terminal tuberculars took refuge in Las Vegas as a last-gasp chance for regaining good health. "Eight or ten of those with tuberculosis have waited too long, and the town forces them into the mountain camps where they die."

In the first months of 1912, O'Malley, Taupert, and Plowman, who surely had been appalled by Brown's hostile critique, sat down together to discuss ways to put Las Vegas in a better light. The possibility of landing a world championship prizefight struck them big-time. The three men agreed that such an event would only generate positive things for the city. The trio saw no downside to what they presumed would be an unquestionable master-stroke.

The economic benefits would be many, the men believed. The business-men were certain a world championship would not fail, as so many other city ventures had in the past. Moreover, O'Malley, Taupert, and Plowman were positive that such a consequential event would give Las Vegas a long-standing historic presence.

A prizefight of this magnitude, between two of the best-known sporting figures in America, would forever be remembered for taking place in Las Vegas, New Mexico. Of that, the three men were absolutely sure, with O'Malley, the resident big-time sports bellwether leading the charge. So convinced that the clash would bring lasting prestige to Las Vegas, O'Malley & Company pushed to round up thousands of dollars, much of that from the Las Vegas Athletic Association.

Jack Curley was clearly gladdened that the fight now had financial backing. Curley, however, soon had other problems.

CHAPTER 5

Ladies' Man

JACK CURLEY HAD a way of turning the world heavyweight championship prizefight into a story not about two combatants but about himself. A week and some days after Curley arrived in Las Vegas on May 1, newspapers in Denver were abuzz that he would soon be married to Marie Drescher of Denver.

On May 16, a *Denver Post* report mentioned that Curley would wed later that month and that the bride-to-be and her parents were already making plans to be on their way to Las Vegas.

Early news accounts revealed that the couple would recite their vows not in a church but at Flynn's training site.[1] The boxing ring inside the onetime casino would have to be dismantled and the medicine balls and heavy punching bags pushed aside or, better yet, pushed out of sight.

All things considered, a gymnasium hardly seemed the proper venue to exchange sacred pledges.

Miss Drescher was described in newspapers as a "popular young society belle of Denver, and the daughter of a wealthy and influential family." Not the kind of young woman one might expect to see in a bridal gown inside a workout space heavy with the scent of perspiration.

This was not some long, drawn-out affair, readers soon learned. The couple had met in late April, when Curley and Flynn were in Denver where the Fireman put on a boxing exhibition. Apparently the initial meeting was a case of love at first sight.

Before the Flynn team left Colorado, Curley proposed and Miss Drescher accepted. Curley had been introduced to his intended by Jack Kelly of St. Louis, the city where the Dreschers had lived before they relocated to Denver. According to newspaper statements, the Dreschers were "wealthy

Denver society folk," and Curley and Miss Drescher were absolutely smitten with each other. Marie Drescher was barely eighteen years old and Curley was twice that.

On September 16, 1911, Curley's first wife, Mildred Schul Curley, had been granted a divorce from Curley on the grounds of extreme cruelty. She received a settlement of $22,000. No one seemed particularly bothered by these facts, at least bothered enough to comment publicly.

The Dreschers had planned for their daughter to go to Europe with them before being presented to society. That plan evidently fell apart when Marie met the dashing, prominent, and considerably older Jack Curley.

Curley reportedly had used an automobile belonging to Miss Drescher's parents to court their daughter. The wedding-announcement cards, which circulated in the most fashionable homes of Denver, indicated the groom's name was Armand Schul.[2] Before he came to Denver, Curley had asked a Chicago court to make Jack Curley his legal name. Why his birth name appeared on the announcement information was not explained. Curley was born Jacques Armand Schul, in San Francisco.

From the outset, Curley denied that he would be married in late May.[3] "It is not true. But you can say for me that I wish it were." Meanwhile, Marie Drescher's parents remained discreetly silent. They would neither deny nor confirm the report of a soon-to-be wedding.

A newspaper photograph of Curley and Miss Drescher taken at Colorado Springs seemed to suggest that the engagement was no longer a secret. The *Las Vegas Optic* reported that the couple and her parents would soon be added to the social circles in Las Vegas. Such circles would of course be considerably smaller in circumference than those in Denver.

Miss Drescher and her parents arrived in Las Vegas on May 19. Curley, ever the gentleman, met them at the station. After a dinner at La Castaneda Hotel, they were taken to a cottage that Flynn and his sparring partners used. Why Curley didn't reserve rooms at La Castaneda is not clear. The Castaneda was definitely classy. The majestic lobby had a high ceiling. A low wrap-around porch was a good place to sit if you were a tubercular. Facing the sun was recommended to catch high, dry air and to let strong rays bake and dry a sufferer's chest. A great deal of coughing was heard there as well as frequent throat clearing of sputum, which went into handkerchiefs or, in some cases, over the side of the porch and onto nearby grounds.

Where the Flynn entourage went was a mystery. To do the chauffeuring out to the Montezuma Castle, Curley on this occasion used his own automobile for a change. Following three weeks of courting, the wedding was held May 21 in the parlors of La Castaneda, at eleven o'clock in the morning. Judge D. R. Murray officiated.[4]

The wedding was attended by all members of Flynn's training camp, as well as those involved in plugging the fight. These included H. W. Lanigan and, to a lesser degree, Arthur Greiner. Credential-less and woefully inexperienced, Greiner had recently been appointed secretary to Curley.

Curley had taken an immediate shine to the "dainty little society girl," the *Las Vegas Optic* noted. During Curley's visit to Denver, the couple, it was reported, "were together from morning to night," spinning around Colorado's capital in the Dreschers' automobile.

Dinner at La Castaneda followed the ceremony, attended by a number of notable Las Vegas residents. Ostensibly all were members of the city's social circle. The following afternoon, Curley, his bride, Jim Flynn, and Mr. and Mrs. Drescher traveled to Albuquerque where, on Thursday night, May 23, Flynn would put on a boxing exhibition. For the "wealthy and influential" Drescher parents, such an agenda surely was likely not what they had in mind for their daughter.

All matters involving the prizefight and the newlyweds were going along as well as could be expected. Then, on June 6, the *Denver Post* published an eyebrow-raising piece of news about the private life of Jack Curley, the former Jacques Armand Schul.

Unbeknown to the Drescher family and to many other people, Curley had become involved in a divorce scandal—not his own—back in Chicago. It seemed that love letters written by Curley and by Mrs. E. B. Overshiner were being introduced in a Chicago courtroom by Mrs. Overshiner's husband, who had entered a bill of divorcement against his wife.[5]

The contents of those letters, according to the *Denver Post*, "burn with love messages." Thrown into this sudden and alarming storm, the W. C. Dreschers stood by their new son-in-law. In defending her daughter, Mrs. Drescher told a reporter that Curley was "a man of the world." As such, she added: "He should be forgiven for his transgressions of running around the country with a common-law wife every now and then."[6]

If readers were confused by such disconcerting news, Mrs. Drescher was not yet finished with her rather odd view of things. "I have been given to understand that Mr. Curley, like a great many other men of the world, traveled with a woman sometimes known as his wife."

Mrs. Drescher had one more bit of business to make known. "The woman to whom Mr. Curley was permitted to get a divorce from," she disclosed, "was never married to him." The amount of head scratching that followed that piece of information must had been substantial.

It came as no surprise that Mrs. Drescher's words did not find widespread agreement. The *Santa Fe New Mexican* rejected all explanations surrounding Curley's extramarital activities.

"The letters indicate very low moral ideals in certain circles of the so-called sporting world," the *New Mexican* reported. Meanwhile, the *Rocky Mountain News* termed Curley's deportment "a tarnished romance." The newspaper sniffed that Curley, "in an extreme act of gallantry," was permitted to obtain a divorce from Mrs. Overshiner in order that she might have certain standing in the world."

The letters from Mrs. Overshiner to Curley and vice versa appeared to be more than simple, newsy jottings. "Me for you," Mrs. Overshiner penned in one message. "Yours till the cows come home," Curley signed off in return.

Mrs. Overshiner declared that she had several more letters from Curley, which were not of a nature that is generally accepted as polite correspondence between one man and another man's wife. The wording of these letters indicated that Curley wrote them just prior to his marriage to Marie Drescher. In one of the letters, Curley asks Mrs. Overshiner if she could arrange to meet him in California on June 1, 1912. Curley, wed barely a week, had dispatched this letter from Las Vegas.

Curley told Mrs. Overshiner that he had a nice house in California and that there would be "plenty of room for her if she would only accept his invitation." Was Curley planning to take his bride *and* Mrs. Overshiner with him to California? Such a proposition was not stated.

However, Curley did invite Mrs. Overshiner to Las Vegas, an act that would surely have discombobulated his bride as well as members of that community's social circle.

"This place (Las Vegas) would work wonders for you," the fight promoter wrote, "if you can stand the simple life for a couple of months. It has all the hot springs beaten to death. And I'd do everything I promised you, and treat you like a baby sis. Thanks so much for telling me of your little trouble. Write often and hurry up your plans when I can see you." He signed the letter "J."

In another letter, Mrs. Overshiner asked Curley, "Will you be in Las Vegas all the time up to July 1? Am nearly settled now in my apartment—expect to have some parties here. Will write you more news later." She signed the letter, "Me for you when I get big." Was Florence Overshiner expecting to be impregnated by Jack Curley? Though doubtful, such a notion was certainly not out of the question.

Somehow, Curley, assisted by H. W. Lanigan, pursued the promotion of the fight, which must have been difficult in light of the exposure of Curley's very private matters. And yet Curley surely had much of the country wondering this: "What in God's name is going on out there in far-off New Mexico?"

The exchange of the sizzling letters was simply another bump in the already rutted road that was more and more leading toward a July Fourth botch-up.

Jack Curley's parents were from the Alsace region of France, and had fled from there in the 1870s, heading to the United States to escape reprisals of the Franco-Prussian War. Homesick, they later returned to France, to Strasbourg and Paris, where Curley spent his formative years.

Curley's name came from the curly hair he had as a boy. He grew up to be an ingratiating sort, suave enough from the polished accent that he had gained from time spent *en français*. That voice offset a rather homely face. He dressed well, however, and always seemed to have walking-around money on his person. Moreover, he had contacts across the globe and enjoyed fine dining and the best hotels.

On June 5, Curley and his bride returned from California where he had spent a week in Los Angeles and San Francisco negotiating with motion-picture companies about filming the bout.[7] He also found himself now dealing with the won't-go-away belief that New Mexico's governor, William McDonald, intended to prevent the fight from happening, no matter what. Curley confidently asserted to everyone he met that his opinion was that the fight would take place as scheduled. And yet Curley said that Juarez, Mexico—in a bullfight ring, no less!—would probably be the place the bout would be staged in the event that Las Vegas was scratched.

Ole!

Curley stood his ground by insisting that there was a great amount of interest in the event from the West Coast. However, published comments in various newspapers in June 1912 indicated otherwise. The trip to California was not a honeymoon excursion. That was to be taken after the Johnson-Flynn battle. Curley and his wife, Marie Drescher—not his very good friend Florence Overshiner, or his first wife, or any other woman—were often headed out of town.

On June 18 the Curley group boarded Santa Fe no. 1 in Las Vegas and were bound for Albuquerque to take care of some business. That excursion surely had to do with the prizefight.

Herman Ilfeld, a prominent Las Vegas merchant and trader, a man well versed in matters of commerce, as well as one of the biggest boosters of Las Vegas, joined the couple. Ilfeld happened to be happily married—to one woman. Perhaps Mr. Ilfeld was along to make sure Mr. and Mrs. Jack Curley stayed married.[8]

Meanwhile, the two prizefighters had other things on their minds, such as settling into training camps and preparing for a heavyweight championship war.

CHAPTER 6

A Welcome Mat and a Doormat

ON MAY 9, a brass band and some two hundred people greeted Jim Flynn when he arrived at the Las Vegas train station. The *Albuquerque Morning Journal* couldn't resist printing some catty remarks. "Innocent, unsophisticated Las Vegas not so long ago was populated with gunfighters and injuns. Now residents have the opportunity to gaze for the first time at a man who fights with his fists."

Flynn's assemblage included Jack Curley; Flynn's brother Louis Flynn; H. W. Lanigan; sparring partner Al Williams; A. H. Blake; Flynn's chauffeur; chef Chick Coleman; and a piano player said to noodle the keys as well as Paderewski.

A chef and a pianist were not enough for Flynn, who clearly suffered from grandiosity. To that end, Flynn hired his own personal waiter and bartender, W. K. Luckensmeier. The two men knew each other in Pueblo, where Luckensmeier worked long hours at the busy Sturges Café, a hash house where music was not played, diners were many, and no one ate by candlelight.

Two weeks after Flynn's arrival, Jack Curley journeyed by automobile to a ranch owned by Frank Forsyth, and located six miles from Las Vegas on the Los Alamos Road. Flynn had already set up a temporary residence out by the closed-down Montezuma Castle, seven miles from town. A training site for Johnson had yet to be procured. Curley, who had visited many prospective quarters in Las Vegas, looked over the Forsyth premises and thought them ideal for the Johnson coterie. He found Forsyth, an old-timer to the area, perfectly willing to allow the champion to use his spread as a training camp—gratis.[1]

Always on the lookout for a good bargain, Curley wired Johnson immediately and told him how perfect the ranch was and urged him to reply at once whether the place should be reserved for him. Johnson said he would leave the selection of a training spot to the promoter's judgment, which was not always a good idea.

While Curley waited, the *Albuquerque Morning Journal*, hearing about the Forsyth Ranch, jumped on the bandwagon. "The ranch has many advantages," the newspaper reported. "The buildings are large and roomy, there is plenty of water and a short distance away there is a lake in which there are some excellent bass."

The *Journal* said that Mr. Forsyth was a fancier of high-grade chickens. Forsyth, an Albuquerque reporter went on, "keeps his chicken coop locked at night, but he always kills a couple of fowl for Sunday dinner. He might invite Johnson to join him some him some sunny day on the Sabbath."

This strange sales pitch, surely overseen by Lanigan, continued in its irrationality: "There is also a herd of buffalo nearby. If Johnson felt like tackling a strenuous exercise, he may be allowed to ride one of these critters."

Lanigan's pitch now bordered on insanity. Who in his right mind would want to climb aboard a full-grown bison that tipped the scales at two thousand pounds?

To peddle the idea of a real ranch to Johnson became a daily exercise in the *Morning Journal* as well as in the *Daily Optic*. "Forsyth could spin yarns about gun fights and bad men in the area who once roamed there thick in every locality." The *Optic* boasted that Johnson's fancy buggy would be able to reach town in no time.

As if to close the deal, the *Optic* wrote that Johnson could tell Forsyth about the fights he had had in the ring. What is more, the ranch was several remote miles from the Flynn camp and there would be no danger of the two men meeting each other while out on their long training runs.

Flynn viewed Johnson's delay in showing up as a good thing. Every day that Johnson stayed away from the altitude of Las Vegas, Flynn said, the better the chance he had in defeating the champion. It did not seem to matter to Flynn that the fight was more than a month away, more than enough time to acclimate to an elevation of 6,424 feet.

Johnson finally appeared in Las Vegas, on May 28, along with a training-camp retinue that included his wife, Etta; two white sparring partners, Marty Cutler and Jack DeBray; two black boxers; trainer Watson Burns; a musician; Johnson's chauffeur; and Mrs. Johnson's maid.[2]

Johnson, too, was met at the station by a crowd and a brass band. Like Flynn, Johnson had been in New Mexico before, via train, but this would be the first time he had set foot in the state.

The Johnson cohort was immediately driven to the fighter's training headquarters at the Forsyth Ranch. That's where the real trouble started. As Johnson checked out the Forsyth property, he suddenly threw up his hands in horror and declared the property "the filthiest place [he] have ever seen." Stagnant pools of water were seen in every direction. Rubbish was piled high all around. The house intended for Johnson's attendants was vermin infested. Johnson's trainers declared that even a dog would have no chance under such unsanitary conditions.[3]

A hostelry of great grandeur this was not.

Just as bad were the coyotes that had howled all night to keep Johnson from his needed sleep that first night. In the daytime, things were much too quiet for the champion's taste. The ranch was far from town. As much as he liked driving a car, Johnson didn't like such a distance.

Johnson wanted to be as close as he could to town, where he could see people and they could glimpse him.[4] What's more, he saw no trees at the ranch. Indeed, the Forsyth homestead was surrounded by ground as flat and empty as a cleared plate. The Johnson party spent two days at the Forsyth place. For the world heavyweight champion, that was two days too many.[5]

Soon after dismissing the site, Johnson announced that he would decamp downstate, at Jemez Springs, sixty-four miles west of Albuquerque. Alfredo Otero, a native of that area, reportedly offered the champion a thousand dollars to set up his training quarters there. Johnson would have free use of the area's hot springs, a nice home, and other conveniences if he chose to move in. Johnson turned down the deal without even seeing the spread.

Word of Johnson's search for a training camp quickly brought invitations from near and far. Officials at the Santa Fe Chamber of Commerce urged Johnson to stay in the capital city. Freedom to move about the city and guaranteed ideal quarters were presented. So eager was the Chamber to have this celebrated figure in their midst, Santa Feans told Johnson he could train at the National Guard Armory there. Even better was this unimaginable promise: Johnson's group could pitch tents in the center of Santa Fe's historic downtown plaza.

Eventually, Albuquerque joined in the discussion of a top-notch training camp. The *Morning Journal* wrote that members of the Commercial Club in that city had extended quarters to Johnson free of charge.[6] Surprisingly, Johnson said no. He did agree that he would come to Albuquerque on or about June 19 to put on an exhibition. Johnson later admitted he had heard that Albuquerque hotels were not particularly welcoming to black guests.[7]

Johnson finally chose to live and train at the residence of Francisco Baca y Sandoval. This came with a two-story house and a large yard just off the plaza in Las Vegas.[8] Johnson liked this spot because it was in town, not far out in the wilds. A large porch on the front of the house attracted Johnson. It would let him watch the world go by. Perhaps best of all, Johnson felt sure that coyotes would not be howling in town from midnight until dawn.

Johnson was immensely pleased with his bungalow on the west side of town and laughed at the reports from Albuquerque and Santa Fe that he was planning to vacate this neighborhood and move his possessions a long way off. He liked the idea of settling in a neighborhood "where there would be no stories told" of him "fooling away time."

In the hubbub over a proper place for Johnson, Flynn was busy taking training runs out near Montezuma Castle. Often times he would take his walking stick with him. Why he would run with a walking stick was not entirely clear.

Clear to all was Johnson's upcoming appearance in Santa Fe.

CHAPTER 7

Jack Does Santa Fe

JACK JOHNSON FIRST appeared in New Mexico on May 14, 1912, though that date is not technically accurate.[1] On that night, Santa Fe fans a got a glimpse of the world champion—not in person, but in moving pictures: the silent kind.

These animated pictures were shown at the capital city's Elks Theatre and had been made in Chicago in mid-April. The pictures depicted Johnson and his July the Fourth challenger Jim Flynn.

According to the *Santa Fe New Mexican*, which previewed the show, the pictures revealed the size and speed of the contestants during a variety of training exercises.

The Santa Fe newspaper called the two thousand–plus feet of film "exceedingly interesting." Other critics who saw the pictures, the *New Mexican* reported, proclaimed them to be "interesting and decidedly instructive." Apparently, much of life in the ancient city was "interesting."

The *New Mexican* went on to point out that the pictures would appeal to the ladies as well as to the "sterner sex." The journalist who came up with that line had reportedly learned that sporting events were discussed in homes and surely read about in news reports by every member of the household. That was a good reason, the writer said, why ladies would want to see what "all the fuss was about."

Other theaters in other cities in the United States had already shown the pictures and typically charged the public twenty-five cents. In Santa Fe, the Elks Theater's manager proudly announced that, depending on location of the seat, he would charge only ten or fifteen cents, which were the usual admission amounts at that venue.

New Mexico governor William McDonald and his staff had been extended invitations to witness the performance at the Elks Theatre. It was not known whether the governor or his confidants would accept or decline the offers. The governor, once happy about showcasing the fight, had now spurned it. The bout would, he said, attract numerous flimflammers and scads of reprobates. Though he wasn't an attorney, McDonald mistakenly believed that boxing wasn't legal in New Mexico. He was wrong, of course. And yet he said he would do all he could to keep the fight from happening.

To cope with the criminal element that McDonald spoke of, Las Vegas, guided by Mayor Robert Taupert, ordered more police to be on duty and "all hoboes and shady characters" to be run out of town or, in some cases, jailed. To expedite this plan, Taupert appointed Curley assistant chief of police and presented him with a gold badge.[2]

Johnson was initially promised that he could do an exhibition in Albuquerque. When he realized the lodging there would not accept a black man, Mark Levy, head of the New Mexico Athletic Association, spent a week trying to line up something in Santa Fe.[3] When state legislators stepped in with requests to see that exhibition, the door opened wide and a June 7 date was obtained.[4] Johnson was to box three sparring partners that night, presumably not all at once. This exhibition would also be held at the Elks Theater, on the stage.[5]

A display advertisement in the *Santa Fe New Mexican* announced: "Ladies Especially Invited." Seats were $1 and $1.50. Ringside seats cost $2. Tickets were on sale at Fischer's Drug Store.

"The Lord of Pugdom," as a Santa Fe reporter called Johnson, arrived in the capital city in Johnson's large touring car.[6] With the champion was an entourage that included Johnson's wife, her maid, and Professor Watson Burns, Johnson's chief trainer. Sparring partners George DeBray, Marty Cutler, Kid Skelly, Jack Perkins, and Calvin Respress traveled by train.

Those riding in Johnson's automobile left Las Vegas at 10:00 a.m. They did not reach Santa Fe until 6:00 p.m. The exhibition took place at 9:00 p.m.

DeBray, Cutler, and Skelly were, a local reporter wrote, "perfectly fine-looking physical specimens." He added that, when they stood beside the slightly over six-feet-tall Johnson, "the threesome resembled pygmies."

Before he took the stage at the Elks, Johnson said, "I wish to show the people of Santa Fe that a boxer can be a gentleman. The impression I leave you with is that I desire to be honorable both to myself and to the sport of which I am an exponent."

There was a noticeable lack of brag in Johnson.[7] He then delivered words that he and Flynn would utter regularly during the weeks leading up to the July fight. "In regard to the battle which is coming, I wish to say that I shall do all I can to defeat Jim Flynn. I will use every fair means to that end. Above all, may the best man win."[8]

"May the best man win" would go on to become the most overused and truly meaningless cliché heard throughout the spring and early summer of 1912. Johnson spoke that eternal chestnut the day he arrived in Las Vegas. He clearly knew the identity of the best man.

When Johnson stepped into the ring that had been set up inside the Elks, a local writer could not restrain his awe. "Scientists have pronounced Jack Johnson the norm of physical perfection and certainly it is hard to imagine how his measurements could bring an added iota to his great strength." That same writer then contradicted himself. "He doesn't seem to have an ounce of superfluous flesh on him and his great bulk is truly appalling."

Down this slippery slope of mangled prose the writer merrily went. "The champion is in the best of physical condition to meet the giant railroader." Giant? By most measurements, Flynn stood slightly more than five feet and nine inches tall.

The attendance figure for the exhibition was not given. However, the *Albuquerque Evening Herald*, in a report that unmistakably appeared to be crafted by Lanigan, who did not go to Santa Fe, judged those on hand to be "a large crowd." The site, said the *Herald*, was "packed to the shingles, with standing room being taken to the last inch."

The *Albuquerque Evening Herald* reporter gushed the next day with approval. "Johnson won hundreds of friends by his appearance in Santa Fe. He is a real gentleman all the time. He gave one of the great shows for the Santa Fe people, boxing nine three-minute rounds with three of his trainers and making a speech that was alone worth the price of admission."

While in Santa Fe, the Johnson camp members visited several public buildings, including a tour of the State Penitentiary by special invitation of Warden John H. McManus. For Johnson, seeing jail cells with bars must have been a case of déjà vu. In 1901, he and heavyweight Joe Choynski had spent twenty-three days locked up in a Galveston, Texas, jail for engaging in an unlawful prizefight.[9]

It is not clear where the Johnson party stayed in Santa Fe the night of the exhibition. Perhaps at the Palace Hotel. Lodging in the capitol city was open to black guests. It's possible some of the group took rooms at an inn off the plaza, which later became the celebrated La Fonda Hotel and marked the end of the Santa Fe Trail.[10] The bulk of the group arrived back in Las Vegas in Johnson's big Chalmers automobile late Saturday afternoon. In his pocket Johnson carried $600, his appearance fee for sparring in Santa Fe.[11]

CHAPTER 8

A Familiar Voice

THE VOLUBLE TOMMY Cannon arrived in Las Vegas on May 23. If visitors did not recognize him right away, they likely heard him.

Curley had contracted Cannon to be the ring announcer for the fight. Additionally, Cannon would serve as Lanigan's chief assistant in pitching the bout. Advertising the heavyweight program also fell under Cannon's domain. Likewise, Art Greiner would assist Lanigan, though doing what was not specified.

Wearing several hats at such a major event, as Cannon did, is not something that would happen in this day and age. However, in the spring of 1912, the unusual in Las Vegas swiftly became a part of the landscape.[1]

Born in Mississippi in 1859, Cannon early on was a cotton ginner. Eventually he gravitated toward boxing matches and by 1888 had become a veteran at announcing prizefights. He occasionally served as referee for these shows, but it was his robust vocal cords that brought him notice.

Microphones, or a public-address system, did not show up in boxing rings until many years later.

Newsmen typically described Cannon as "golden throated" or "silver tongued." He preferred to be known as "the little man with the big voice."[2] He had announced fights for John L. Sullivan, Jim Corbett, Bob Fitzsimmons, and Jake Kilrain, among many others. Bombastic and blustery, Cannon visited the Las Vegas training camps and told reporters what he found: "At this stage of the game, Jim Flynn is by far a higher class—looking athlete than Jack Johnson. Johnson is plainly flabby and way overweight.[3] He has got to work hard in the weeks in front of him if he is to be as good a man physically as he was in Reno the day he defeated Jim Jeffries."

Soon after he settled in Las Vegas, Cannon marched into the office of the *Las Vegas Optic*.[4] There he proclaimed, "I have many clever advertising schemes up my sleeve." He expected to begin on one of those schemes immediately, he said, which was a giant billboard. The billboard would be one hundred feet long and fifteen feet high, Cannon explained. The huge sign would stand at a point north of the city and be clearly visible to those coming into Las Vegas on a train from, say, Denver.

Cannon planned to hire someone to paint a picture of the arena and do life-sized portraits of Johnson and Flynn for the billboard. Along the edges of the panels would be advertisements from Las Vegas merchants and other businesses across New Mexico.

The billboard, as with numerous brainstorms conceived during the weeks prior to the prizefight, never happened. Perhaps it was decided that few people would be able to read much of a busy sign while blazing past it in an automobile or a passenger train.

On the one occasion when free advertising did come the fight's way, even that turned into a washout.[5] On May 19, 1912, a Cincinnati newspaper devoted half a page on the front of its Sunday section to the goings-on in Las Vegas. Curiously, there were no articles about the upcoming prizefight in this spread. Nor were there feature articles about Johnson and Flynn. Instead, there was a bizarre assortment of photographs. Rather than showing a photo of Flynn or Johnson sparring, one photo pictured Curley, George Tripp, and Charles O'Malley posing together. Another shot was of Al Tearney, the not-particularly-well-known stakeholder for the world championship.

There were images too of El Porvenir and La Castaneda hotels. However, there was no accompanying information in the photographs about available rooms, rates, or amenities, or even about how to make reservations or obtain a ticket.

Strangest of all in this mélange was a close-up of the front of the San Miguel National Bank in Las Vegas. What southern Ohio newspaper readers would think of a bank 1200 miles away is hard to imagine. One thing is certain: Tommy Cannon had no part of this "scheme." Clearly, someone—Art Greiner, perhaps—should have followed the photographer around and made suggestions. But that did not happen, which likely surprised no one.

During Cannon's time in Las Vegas, he was interviewed by a young reporter with the *Kansas City Star*. The rookie journalist wrote that Cannon was "silver-voiced." It's entirely possible that the reporter had never actually heard Cannon in a prizefight ring. During that interview Cannon said he would be a "shillaber" for the Las Vegas fight. In days gone by a shillaber was an employee of the circus who rushed up to the box office the moment a barker concluded his pitch. He and his fellow shillabers would purchase tickets and swiftly head inside the tent, with a crowd now eagerly following. Much later a shillaber was more commonly known as a "shill."

Cannon gave the youthful *Star* writer a sample of his shillaber spiel: "Thousands will be on hand July the Fourth to hear me announce, Jack Johnson, the king of all pugilistic exhibitors, and Jim Flynn, the most intrepid warrior that ever graced the center of the squared circle. Got that, kid? 'Squared circle?' I've got it copyrighted."[6]

Today's well-known ring announcer Michael Buffer threatens to file suit against anyone using his familiar "Let's get ready to rumble!" before a fight. Chances are very good that Cannon did not possess legal ownership of "squared circle."

Cannon told the Kansas City cub reporter that he had watched Flynn "work like a hero," and Jack Johnson "stall like a capper." He let the freshman scribe know he had the dope down—"so fine that you will almost soak your watch to get a bet down."

"Johnson," Cannon crowed, "is the greatest thing that ever shoved the brown leather." The veteran announcer quickly backtracked and admitted that, being on the Curley payroll, he would have to give the nod to the Fireman at the outcome.

"I used to think that Flynn was a mutt until I came to Las Vegas and got my own eyes full," Cannon said. He had expected to gaze upon "an ossified souse," but instead saw a coming champion. "Flynn has improved 100 percent. His heart is big as an Oregon apple."

According to Cannon, Flynn was not hesitant to tell how he was going to win. "He's going to dig in and make all the white folks happy," the *Kansas City Star* dutifully reported.

Cannon, who somehow knew the fight's finances, said the proceedings of the event were going along terrifically, which was hardly the case. "The fight will draw at least $200,000," the announcer boasted. "Flynn and Curley will take down enough to spend the balance of their lives racing around in six-cylinder machines. It's going to be a great show."

CHAPTER 9

On the Road with the Fireman

ON MAY 22, Jim Flynn, Jack Curley, and Al Williams, Flynn's chief sparring partner, climbed aboard Santa Fe no. 1 in Las Vegas and headed south. With them were Marie Drescher Curley, the promoter's bride of one day; her parents, Mr. and Mrs. W. C. Drescher; and Mr. and Mrs. Arthur Greiner.

Flynn had been to Albuquerque before. He had stopped in the city in 1902 and went a few rounds in Old Town for the benefit of fans. He wasn't remembered for showing even a modicum of championship class.[1]

Coincidentally, in 1909, Flynn had fought an Albuquerque black man named Bill Pettus.[2] Like Jack Johnson, Pettus was a native Texan. This tussle took place not in New Mexico but in Pueblo, Colorado. Flynn easily earned the victory by punishing Pettus, closing the black man's left eye early and then adding to the pounding.[3]

The idea of having Flynn show up for an exhibition in Albuquerque was conceived in late April. Promoter Jack Curley sent a letter to Mark Levy, the director of the New Mexico Athletic Club. In Albuquerque, Flynn was set to put on an exhibition that would, Curley hoped, let people see the challenger in the flesh and at the same time extol the upcoming fight. Apparently the Drescher women were happy just to be along on the ride.

Curley must have been a little uneasy about this visit. Only three days before, he had announced that the Johnson-Flynn fight would be held on the morning of July 4.

Fans did not like that plan one single bit. To get to Las Vegas, Albuquerque spectators would be forced to take a dawn train. Meanwhile, ticketholders from Trinidad, Raton, and various places to the north would have to arrive in the afternoon the day before and take a train back north following the fight.

Curley's reasoning for a morning fight was that Johnson and Flynn would be in better condition in the early part of the day, rather than at midday or at night. It must be remembered that Curley had never worn boxing gloves in his life and was promoting his first prizefight.

Johnson and Flynn surely were against a morning bout. The two fighters liked to sleep in, and Johnson, for one, often returned home in the wee hours after taking part in spirited craps games or lively sessions making music until the sun began to take a peek at the carrying-on. It took almost three weeks for Curley to come to his senses and declare that the fight would not be held in the morning but at two o'clock in the afternoon.[4]

Flynn's Albuquerque agenda was not simply to box a few rounds with Williams. The challenger was on hand to attend the national convention of the Brotherhood of Locomotive Firemen and Enginemen, which happened to be held at the same time in New Mexico's largest city.[5] A veteran with the big coal scoop, Fireman Flynn still held on to his membership card in that organization, even though he was now a prizefighter of long standing.

To greet Flynn's arrival at the Albuquerque depot, the Duke City Band, led by conductor Ben Disneo, struck up the familiar "For He's a Jolly Good Fellow."[6] As the musicians played on, the Flynn group attempted to make its way toward the city's showpiece, the Alvarado Hotel. The crowd was so large that Santa Fe Railroad officials and city policemen had to be called on to help the challenger and his team reach the front steps of the hotel.

Onlookers stampeded across the hotel's lawns and onto the veranda to get a glimpse of the Fireman. The great throng, wrote a hyperexcited reporter for the *Albuquerque Morning Journal*, was "packed as thick as the thicket of a football scrimmage."

Another newspaperman, similarly caught up in the thrill of the event, ludicrously estimated the Albuquerque turnout to be greater and grander than appearances in the city by William H. Taft and Theodore Roosevelt, back when those two sitting presidents paid separate visits to Albuquerque.[7]

When Flynn reached the front of the gathering, J. Porter Jones, a well-to-do businessman who had a high position at the local Buick automobile dealership, told him, "Say something to them, Jim."

"What will I say?" Flynn asked.

"Anything," Jones replied.

A first-class grouch, Flynn snapped, "You talk to them."

"No, they want to hear you, Jim," Jones calmly answered.

Lanigan apparently had not prepared a speech beforehand and thus Curley came to the rescue. Flynn's manager moved to face the surge of people and shouted, "I'm very glad to meet you all."

A victim of flop sweat, Flynn eventually stepped forward and admitted to the crowd that he wasn't a speechmaker. He was holding a walking stick that appeared to be a cane. Had he been hurt? Not at all. He often hiked about Las Vegas with the stick. He had brought it along on this outing to use as a crutch-like prop. To emphasize a point, Flynn took the stick in one hand and smacked it on the palm of his other hand.

"I am confident I will beat the Negro." Thwack!

"I am going to get the championship title back for the white race." Thwack!

"Get it back where it belongs." Thwack!

Much cheering followed those words and bystanders were careful to not accidentally come in contact with the stick.

When Flynn finished talking, William McIntosh, a wealthy sheep man and rancher from central New Mexico, worked his way forward to address the Fireman.[8]

"I've got a thousand dollar bet on you and I think I'm going to lose."

"All right," said Flynn, "I'll take that bet off your hands. Where's it posted?"

"I think I'm going to lose," McIntosh repeated.

"Wait," said Flynn. "I'll take your bet, take it right now and pay thirty dollars for it besides."

"That so?" McIntosh said.

"You bet it is," Flynn said.

"I'll take it," the sheep man said.

"Where is it?" Flynn asked again.

McIntosh then reached around and grabbed Mark Levy by the arm. "That good?"

"Yes," said Levy to Flynn. "I'll fix this for you."

Flynn appeared satisfied. To show so, he raised his stick and brought it down hard on the palm of his other hand.

Thwack!

That night Flynn and Al Williams went four rounds against each other at the Elks Theater in Albuquerque. Because neither man desired to hurt the other, both wore five-ounce gloves.[9]

These were smaller and lighter than normal gloves. The audience on hand watched the action carefully, trying to judge what Flynn would be like against Johnson. The reaction was mixed. Some spectators felt Flynn was a good infighter and would be able to stand a great amount of punishment. Others believed Flynn was not big enough and not skilled enough to slip a knockout punch past Johnson.

A few weeks before the Albuquerque exhibition, Mark Levy had invited aspiring heavyweights in Albuquerque, or from the city's environs, who wished to meet Flynn to come to the office of the New Mexico Athletic Association. The invitation was not simply to pat the Puebloan on the back. It was to box against Flynn.

Anyone was welcome to go one round or up to ten rounds with the Fireman. Nothing came of Levy's offer, which probably was a good thing.

Mark Levy was a workhorse. He would spend ten days in Santa Fe setting up an exhibition for Johnson there. At the last moment Levy took care of ticket sales. Levy also had appeared before the state legislature in Santa Fe, which at the time was debating the Tripp fight bill. George Tripp, a congressman from San Miguel County, had sponsored the measure, which would legalize prizefighting. Levy of course had spoken in favor of it.

Prior to Flynn's visit to Albuquerque, the Orpheum Theater had shown moving pictures of Flynn in training for his fight with Johnson. He boxed, tossed a medicine ball here and there, and did a smattering of roadwork. He also wrestled one of his training partners, which likely confused many in the audience.[10]

Also on the big screen was footage of Johnson leaving his Chicago residence and climbing into his French 120-horsepower racing car. Once seated, Johnson zipped along at breakneck speed, and then skidded the car this way or that, grinning at the camera. Those in the Orpheum did not know whether to laugh or sit still. A few cheers could be heard.

A large group of attendees at the firemen's convention journeyed to Traction Park, which that week was holding a harness-racing program. Flynn, who liked to lay down a bet on anything with four legs, spent a good part of one afternoon at the track living the life of a railbird.

During Flynn's stay in Albuquerque, Barney Oldfield, the most famous race-car driver of that era, happened to stop in the city's train station by chance.[11] Oldfield, Flynn, and Curley visited for half an hour. Oldfield was coming from the West Coast and was headed to Indianapolis where he would attend the Memorial Day race.

Oldfield had hopes of being reinstated as a driver, or perhaps filling in as a reserve driver. He had been suspended for "outlaw racing." Art Greiner, once a race-car driver, was also present at the train station. For some peculiar reason, the *Las Vegas Optic* called Greiner the "society queen" of the Flynn outfit.

One of those unsanctioned races that Oldfield took part in was against Jack Johnson. Johnson, in fact, had challenged Oldfield to a match race at Sheepshead Bay, in Brooklyn, New York, in October 1910. Johnson had lost badly.

Like Flynn, Oldfield did not care for Johnson, mostly because of his skin color. Oldfield happened to be a personal friend of Jim Jeffries. The race-car driver hated that a black man had sent Jeff to the floor.

Oldfield had been barred from the American Automobile Association for participating in that competition with Johnson. At Indianapolis, Oldfield hoped to gain reinstatement in the AAA and be permitted to drive a race car in the 500.

Oldfield's parting words to Flynn were "Do to Johnson as I did at Sheepshead Bay." With that, the Flynn group returned to Las Vegas and to training camp.

CHAPTER 10

Some Sweat, Lots of Play

NO TWO PRIZEFIGHTERS could have more contrasting training camps than Jack Johnson and Jim Flynn. The Johnson camp was relaxed as a cat in the sun. Interruptions came typically when Johnson took off in his touring car, made music, rolled dice, or played pitch for money with members of his crew.

On the other hand, the Flynn camp appeared all business and very little frivolity. Flynn didn't allow gambling in his camp. He finally relented and let his men play poker, but only if they used matchsticks for money.

Some critics thought Johnson's camp too laid back. "He is supposed to be taking long runs in the mornings, but few have seen him at work," one reporter wrote.[1] "His cellar is filled with choice liquors and the popping corks may be heard outside his quarters at almost any hour."[2]

The *Las Vegas Optic* of May 30 said there was little excitement going on in either the Flynn or Johnson camps. Instead came this prosaic report: "Both men are living on the best digestible foods and are sleeping ten or eleven hours each night."

Not to suggest that the two training camps were completely dull. For Flynn, a commotion seemed to occur whenever he did roadwork on the dirt stretches that led from his camp at Montezuma Hot Springs to downtown Las Vegas.

First came the day that Flynn, in the midst of his training gallop, was stopped by the local police.[3] The officer in charge apparently mistook the Fireman for a patient who had escaped from the nearby state insane asylum. Such a mistake aroused great amusement for many who in fact had always considered the fractious Flynn a bit teched, especially when annoyed.

The roadwork incident on June 2 made national news.[4] Several different papers published illustrations that showed a cop waving a billy club in the air while giving chase to a man on foot wearing jail stripes. Such depictions were surely hilarious to everyone, save for Flynn.

Then there was the night Flynn did the chasing, on that same road but now in a blinding rainstorm. On this occasion, he was pursuing, of all people, his chauffeur. The driver had apparently done something that had greatly displeased the Fireman.[5] This tirade also drew laughs nationwide. Could anything else go wrong? Yes. In late May an unexpected snowfall cut short the Fireman's roadwork.

Flynn could sprint at a good clip, but he probably exaggerated his long-distance speed when speaking of it in his camp to reporters. He announced that he could cover ten miles in sixty-five minutes. It's not clear if anyone clocked him. Johnson, meanwhile, cared little for roadwork. One chief way he used to unwind at his camp was by shooting a twenty-two-caliber rifle. He seemed to enjoy that a lot more than trotting up and down pathways or slugging away at punching bags.

Now and then Johnson took off in his car to shoot prairie dogs. On June 15, he drove to the Ten Lakes area, about twenty miles to the northeast of Las Vegas. There he fired away at waterfowl for an hour or two, before his car got stuck in the mud.

For the Johnsons, life proved tranquil in Las Vegas. He trained, but not nearly as much or as hard as he did in earlier days. Las Vegas residents seemed amused. The local newspaper wrote that "he whizzes about in his huge touring car with a large rah-rah hat turned up in front."

One day a promising young fighter named Harry Wills appeared on the scene, seeking a spot as a sparring partner. Wills got cocky and tried to nail Johnson with a right, which the champion grabbed as one reaches out and catches a baseball.[6]

Frequently Johnson would set up empty beer bottles in his Las Vegas yard and attempt to break as many as he could. For all the shooting he did, Johnson was definitely not the best shot around.[7] One morning he and a few of his training-camp confreres set up fixed targets in his yard.

When Johnson's turn to fire came, he accidentally sent a bullet from his rifle through the window of a neighboring house belonging to Mrs. Trinidad Sena. The shell struck a towel rack on the wall of her home, glanced off, and caught Mrs. Sena on the left arm. Fortunately, the force of the bullet had slowed and did not puncture the woman's flesh.[8]

Coincidentally, the Las Vegas Gun Club had scheduled a professional and amateur gathering in late June 1912. Shooters from all over the Southwest would be coming to test their skills with each other. Presumably, Johnson's companions talked him out of taking part.

Yet Johnson did keep a firearm close at hand. As the fight day drew nigh, one morning Johnson found a threatening note on the doorstep of his Gonzales Street house. "Lay Down Nigger on Thursday or We'll String You Up," the message said. It was signed "KKK."[9]

After that, Johnson tucked a revolver in his pants and hired an armed guard to patrol his yard at night, just as he had done in Reno before he fought Jeffries. Fortunately, he never had to squeeze the trigger of the handgun.[10]

Flynn did not pick up a rifle or a firearm of any kind, at least during his stay in Las Vegas. Shooting was not a pastime for him. Flynn did, however, announce that if he lost to Johnson, he would ask this of Jack Curley: "Please shoot me in the head." To referee Ed Smith, the Puebloan made a similar appeal: "I'll give any man in the country full permission to shoot me if I don't win. Honestly, I want to be numbered among the dead ones should Johnson put me down for the count."

Though Jack Johnson grew up in cities, fields and streams beckoned. He liked to fish as well as to shoot. Once again he would drive to Ten Lakes. He liked sitting on a rock near the shoreline and waiting for a tug on his line. Doing so was for the champion a great release.

Despite a beautiful mountain waterway that lay in sight of the Flynn camp, trout fishing was not on the challenger's agenda. "None of that fishing for me," Flynn told reporters. Nonsensical as it might seem, Flynn believed that fishing—and not Johnson's fists—caused Jeffries to drop to the canvas in Reno. Spending a good amount of time sitting still, Flynn said, caused Jeffries to slow down once he entered the ring. Never mind that Jack Johnson that afternoon in Nevada had slowed Jeffries to a complete halt by delivering a brutal boxing lesson to the former champion.

Flynn may have refrained from gunplay in Las Vegas, but that did not stop him from showing his expertise as a trapper, a sort of latter-day mountain man who happened to hail from a blue-collar city.

It seems that Flynn particularly enjoyed eating chicken, often on the days he trained and always on the days he fought. In fact, he was raising fowl outside the cottage where he stayed at Montezuma Hot Springs. The number of birds, Flynn noticed one day, appeared to be lessening. His chef, Chick Coleman, pleaded not guilty.[11]

To find out why this was happening, Flynn set up a trap near his cottage. Lo and behold one morning he discovered he had caught a young polecat of good size.[12]

A small uproar could be heard in Johnson's camp when fans learned he was charging ten cents to anyone wishing to watch the champion train in the thirty-by-thirty-foot wooden platform for a ring that he had brought with him from Chicago and set up in his yard.

When it was announced that the fee had gone up to fifteen cents, this still didn't keep people away. Johnson eventually posted that the price would be a quarter on weekends. Soda pop and chewing gum were also available—for a cost, of course.

Newspapermen were not required to pay to see Johnson toil up close. Spectators who watched Flynn get in shape were far fewer in number than those who shelled out for a glance of the champion. That may be why Flynn did not demand anyone to see him spar or hurl about a medicine ball. There was, too, the distance factor of his camp. Montezuma Hot Springs was a good deal farther away from town than Johnson's training site.

Johnson considered himself a very good baseball player. So good that one afternoon he gathered members of his training camp and challenged the local team, the Las Vegas Maroons, to a game. Before the contest started, Johnson noticed a sign on the wooden fence in the outfield of the Las Vegas ballpark. The sign for Bachrach's Clothing Store indicated that anyone who knocked a baseball over the fence would win a pair of new shoes from Bachrach's. So confident was Johnson about gaining some free dress shoes, he immediately went to the store and had a clerk measure him for a pair.

That wooden fence in Las Vegas bore more than advertising signs. It had several holes in it. A few members of the Maroons apparently feared that Johnson, tall for his time and blessed with oxen strength, might slug a home run through one of those fence openings. Using great caution, a handful of ballplayers for the Maroons went out one night and repaired the fence. So much for Johnson's shoes.

Flynn liked to play handball in the gym at his camp. Full of braggadocio, he announced that he was so good he would take on anyone. When he wasn't playing handball, Flynn pummeled a three-hundred-pound bag filled with oats that hung from a rafter inside the casino.

A peculiar photograph in the *Pueblo Star-Journal* newspaper on June 2 showed Flynn sitting atop a horse. Evidently, he rode a horse now and then in Las Vegas to keep in shape. The caption said, "The Pueblo fireman can be seen galloping over the roads on his mustang." A fight trainer today would never let one of his charges go near a horse, much less a saddle.

A great hullabaloo in the Johnson camp occurred June 2. In the midafternoon rain started to come down heavily.[13] Downpours were frequent visitors in Las Vegas during the late spring and early summer. On this day, several dozen spectators raced about seeking shelter during the sudden cloudburst. The fans soon headed for a large covered balcony fixed to the front of Johnson's house. The balcony was approximately ten feet off the ground. Under the weight of so many bodies, the floor of the overhang creaked and groaned and then went down in a resounding crash. Several women and small boys were among those on the deck during this contretemps. All in attendance agreed it was a miracle that someone was not hurt or seriously injured. Just as astonishing, no one asked for their money back.[14]

That Johnson liked his sleep was well known. One night two of his training-camp attendants got into an argument that kept the champion wide awake. He finally got up and placed big padded gloves on each man. With that, Johnson told them to go to it and not lay down on the job. Johnson acted as referee, and he refused to stop the bout.

The Johnson camp was fun loving. At eleven o'clock one morning, Johnson presided over a kangaroo court. Tom Flanagan, the self-appointed "sheriff," brought upward of two dozen "criminals"—mostly newspaper reporters—before Judge Johnson. The men were found guilty of "hanging around the camp." The usual form of punishment meted out by Judge Johnson at his camp was to give each fellow a spanking with a wide plank. Instead, this time, Johnson ordered his sheriff to cut in half neckties worn by various newsmen and other well-known sporting folk.

At night Johnson would frequently leave his camp and go to the depot to hear the shillabers, who showed up whenever a train arrived. The task for shillabers, who beat on tin pans, was to coax travelers toward commercial stores in Las Vegas.

"I just drop down to see if I can see anyone from Chicago," Johnson said. "I like to hear them beat on the tin pans." Now and then Johnson himself became a shillaber. When a passenger train arrived, he would occasionally get aboard and sell for a dime a postcard that bore his face and signature. Born penny-poor, Johnson never turned down the smallest amount of money.

Flynn typically stayed put in his camp at night. Often he used that time to sit at a table in his cottage and write a letter to his mother. The piano player from Pueblo that he had hired would frequently keep him company.

The two Las Vegas training camps were where Johnson and Flynn issued the most preposterous remarks in the time running up to the fight. "I'll beat Flynn in sixteen rounds," Johnson announced.[15] "After that I'll take on all these 'Hopes' as fast as they can chuck 'em into the ring. I'll lick that bunch in six months and then I'll retire and never fight again."[16]

Periodically, Johnson would reword this promise. He would win in twelve rounds, he predicted, then nine. He would retire on Labor Day after knocking out every White Hope. More than once he said, "I'm like Alexander the Great. I'm too good. After I whale Flynn, there isn't anyone else to lick. Then it will be curtains for Jack."

Repeatedly Flynn issued to reporters at his camp a shopworn line about his own mortality. "I'll beat Johnson in the ring or die in the ring."[17] The challenger said his death would not necessarily come from a thumping by Johnson. Rather, Flynn said his demise would be the result of pistol shots from Curley and others to whom Flynn had given directives.

More than one newspaperman noticed that Flynn appeared to be a misanthrope, accountable to no one. Those same reporters saw Johnson go out of his way to make friends with all sorts in Las Vegas. The way he sauntered along Las Vegas streets resembled a presidential candidate moving slowly past a crowd. He bowed and waved right and left, as would a real friend of the people.

Flynn cared little what people thought of him personally. In fact, he often snarled at visitors at his camp. This concerned Curley, who wanted tickets to be sold. Being irascible was not good publicity at all.

When asked by reporters about his weight and why he was heavier now than before, Flynn said, "Because I haven't smoked a cigarette in ten months." (Not true.) "Nor have I taken a drink of liquor in a year and a half." (Also likely untrue.) Photographs taken in Hot Springs in April indicated there was plenty to drink at the hotel. Some pictures taken there showed Flynn puffing away on a cigarette.

On June 6, the improbable came about.[18] Johnson gathered a handful of people, including a reporter, from his training camp and ushered them into his car. He informed his passengers that he was headed to Flynn's base of operations.

"Surely you are not going near him," Mrs. Johnson said in genuine alarm.

"Why not?" Johnson answered.

There was talk that this kind of visit had never happened before in the long history of heavyweight prizefighting. When he reached Montezuma, Johnson stopped his car as soon he saw Flynn and a few of his bodyguards sitting on the porch of his cottage.

"Hello, Fireman," the champion called as his car came to a stop.

"Hello, Champ," said Flynn as he dropped the newspaper he was reading and clomped down the porch steps to greet the man he would exchange punches with on July the Fourth.

"Came to look you over and see what sort of place you have," Johnson said. "Gee, what a dandy spot. Wish I had beat you to it. If a man can't get in shape here, he's a hopeless case."

"That's the way I feel," Flynn said.

The two men chatted amiably and then walked up the hill to Flynn's gym, which Johnson looked over admiringly. They parted with another handshake.

Later that night, Johnson spoke to those at his camp: "The time has passed when two men, matched to battle in the ring, should be enemies out of the ring. Flynn is a good soul and I like him."[19]

Perhaps the most curious difference between the two training camps was, of all things, rope skipping. Johnson did not believe in it at all. He was sure it injured the action of a man's heart.[20] Had he checked with a medical doctor about such a belief? Probably not. Flynn on the other hand was a firm believer in jumping rope as a means of developing a man's legs and helping his general speed, which sounded more rational.

Bert Smith of the *Los Angeles Daily Times* had the opportunity to spend time in both men's training centers and thus make comparisons.[21] At Jim Flynn's setup, Smith learned that the challenger had recently knocked out one of his sparring partners, a nascent lightweight named Kid Skelton.

Barely nineteen years old, Skelton claimed that Flynn hit him as they were shaking hands.[22] Flynn said Skelton head-butted him. Smith decided to set the record straight. In Flynn's desire to show off, Smith wrote, the fighter had pounded the inexperienced youth in front of a large crowd. Informed of the situation, Smith was filled with disgust.

Without waiting to give Flynn another chance, Skelton quit the Fireman. The next day the young man was hired by Johnson as a sparring partner. Skelton was quite happy with this change. He told Smith that in terms of boxing skills there were no similarities between the two prizefighters.

Flynn would be no match for the black champion. Smith wrote that Flynn was overweight, had a swelled head, and was habitually cantankerous. On the other hand, Johnson had an outsized personality, Smith discovered. Johnson's camp, Smith saw, was amicable and certainly a lot less hostile than Flynn's congregation.[23]

Johnson gave a short, impromptu speech to Smith on June 1. He would knock down Flynn in the tenth round, he said, and put him away for good in the eleventh. Smith also took time to watch Mrs. Johnson. "A beautiful woman," he wrote of her. "She took an interest in the workouts of her husband."

Johnson had seven sparring partners on his dole. "It is a collection," Smith wrote, "that would make the Sultan of Sulu envious."

One day Smith observed Johnson tearing into a punching bag with such force that the leather came loose from its straps. Part of the bag hit a sporting writer in the stomach. Johnson swiftly apologized. A more agreeable prizefighter, Smith said, he had never witnessed. If it were not for Johnson's color, Smith decided, the black man would be the most popular man who ever entered a boxing ring.

Smith wrote, "Flynn is gracious to newspapermen but to others he is lofty and dictatorial. He thinks the world revolves around his camp."

On June 9, the upheaval meter in Flynnville suddenly rose several more degrees. Al Williams, who had trained with the Fireman since Hot Springs, suddenly quit the camp. He walked into town and said he was done and was going to California, his home state. "Me for Frisco and in a hurry," he explained. "I don't even want to be near the Flynn party."

For the Flynn camp, trouble was only beginning.

CHAPTER 11

Two Little Words

DURING THE LONG history of the human race, it is possible that no one walking around save for Tommy Ryan gained so much newspaper ink by saying so very little.

As a prizefighter, Ryan won world championships as both a middleweight and a welterweight. Born in 1870 in upstate New York, and christened Joseph Youngs, Ryan, as did a great many boxers, changed his name in an attempt to show he was Irish, which he wasn't, nor did he look it. At that time, Irish fighters were wildly popular. Not only were they considered fearless, but they carried a reputation for being tough as a dime steak.

When his prizefighting career came to a close, Ryan turned into a savvy trainer, whose students included the renowned Jim Jeffries. So able was Ryan at schooling fighters that journalists took to calling him the "Sage of Syracuse."

Jack Curley had known Ryan for two decades. He had watched Ryan in the ring and outside it. In early 1912, the two agreed to meet in Toronto to talk. Believing Ryan was the right person to turn Jim Flynn into the world's best heavyweight, Curley hired the Sage of Syracuse then and there.

When news spread that Ryan was coming to New Mexico to put Jim Flynn through his paces, writers turned giddy with pleasure. Ryan seemed the gold standard of all trainers and no reporter could wait to write about what Ryan would do for Flynn.

"Tommy to the Rescue," one headline read.

Ryan's train chugged into Las Vegas on May 26. Though he hadn't done a minute of work yet, his reputation was so large that fight fans clogged the station.

"Ryan knows as much about the Johnson uppercut as Johnson does, and more about a lot of other punches," wrote the *Milwaukee Journal*. "He'll teach the Fireman to block every sort of punch before he gets through, and Flynn will be trying to block all the time, for Ryan can still hit."

Without further explanation, Ryan announced that Flynn had a good chance of winning.[1] He said he thought Flynn's "squatty build" was admirable for a battle with Johnson. He liked his pupil's nerve. He admired the Fireman's fast, short uppercuts.

To regular readers of the American press, it must have seemed that every time Tommy Ryan sneezed in Las Vegas, the very act made news. Some examples: Ryan came downtown to look for a place to live for himself and Mrs. Ryan, who would soon be along. Ryan rented a house at 722 Grand Avenue. Ryan went shopping for food at Ike's Grocery. Ryan sparred two rounds with Flynn.

Sport followers will be glad to know that Ryan and his pupil Flynn have already become close, claimed the *Las Vegas Optic*.[2] "They have become as close as members of the same college fraternity."

The *Optic* went on to say, "It was feared by some that the two would not get along nicely and that Flynn might not take kindly to the advice offered him by his trainer-in-chief. On the contrary, Flynn didn't appear to mind when Ryan ordered him around and or talked back." Was such praise accurate?

"Flynn's condition suits me," Ryan said. "He is the most healthy and rugged man I ever saw in my life. He assures me that he weighs at least 215 pounds and if that is the case the public can rest assured he will make 200 pounds by July the Fourth. Fifteen pounds at most is all he has to take off."[3]

By mid-June, whispers about Flynn and Ryan not getting along began to flutter across Las Vegas and eventually the nation.[4] Curley, it was said, was not altogether for keeping Ryan around because Flynn and Ryan seemed to be bickering.[5] Flynn apparently had his own ways to train for an important fight. He was of the temperament that brooked no interference. Here and there were reports of spats up at the Montezuma Castle.

Three weeks into training, real trouble between Ryan and Flynn came to the fore. Ryan had brought Howard Morrow, a light heavyweight, to the Montezuma camp to spar with Flynn. Flynn tried to punch the daylights out of Morrow and then went at Ryan. Heated words ensued. Flynn talked back to Ryan and Ryan stormed off.

The *Milwaukee Journal* had this to say: "Ryan refuses to train anybody unless he, Ryan, is the master."

On June 18, Ryan made an announcement that surely stopped the newspaper-reading public in their tracks: "Am disgusted with Flynn. He is hog fat and has no chance whatever with Johnson. I refuse to have my name used any further in connection with this affair and am leaving camp tonight."

"Hog fat!" The term seemed to leap off the sports page like a battle cry. During the following week and more, those two wee words, six letters in all, took on a life of their own. Indeed, the words overshadowed the very fact that Ryan was now out, finished with Flynn, kaput and done with New Mexico and vice versa.[6]

Reporters would not let go of the two words. In fact, "hog fat" became almost as familiar as the phrase "Remember the *Maine*." Those three words recalled the mysterious explosion of the battleship *Maine* in Havana harbor in 1898. That event propelled the United States into a war with Spain.

Fighters and trainers everywhere mulled "hog fat." Saloon habitués argued about the words. Newspaper perusers lapped up the words because then, as now, many Americans had concerns about taking on surplus poundage themselves. But hog fat? That seemed extreme.

Some writers agreed, that yes, Flynn did seem to present in newspaper photographs some excess avoirdupois. A photo of Flynn was titled "Jim Is Fat." Was Flynn truly fat? The photograph in question showed a shirtless Flynn with a noticeable swollen belly.[7]

Johnson had his own issues with weight. One photograph taken in Las Vegas showed him sitting down. He is wearing a large and billowy shirt that might be of use on a small sailboat. His chest beneath the shirt clearly revealed what are known today as "man boobs."

In time, Ryan had a good deal more to say. "The reason why I resigned from the Flynn camp was that after seeing Flynn train, I was being used merely for the purpose of making Flynn appear to have a chance to beat Johnson."

Ryan continued: "The more I saw of Flynn, the less I thought of him as a fighter. And I came to the conclusion that Flynn had no chance to beat Johnson. That he is too small and too light and knows absolutely nothing about fighting. Flynn is a slugger, pure and simple. Thus, he need not weigh more than 175 pounds."

According to Ryan, Flynn had a very short reach and a bad disposition. "I could not tell him anything, let alone teach him. He can't win. As a white man, I wish to see Flynn come out on top and hope I am mistaken."

During their meeting in Toronto, Curley had proposed that Ryan train Flynn for a certain amount of money, and Ryan accepted the sum. After he saw Flynn perform in Las Vegas, Ryan told Curley that Flynn had no chance of defeating Johnson. Curley said that everyone in the camp had to take a chance on the gate. Curley had tied up so much money for expenses that Ryan could not see his way through on the fight. Curley scoffed at Ryan's proclamation.

"Sour grapes," the promoter said.[8]

Numerous sports writers blamed Ryan's departure on his desire to work solely with Morrow. In fact, during his time in Las Vegas, Ryan managed to line up a fight in Mexico for the promising young fighter.

More than one journalist wrote that Ryan was not the trainer he thought he was. Criticism of Ryan could be found in his own New York backyard. The sporting editor of the *Buffalo Enquirer* called Ryan a "crank" who would not take advice. "He is a second Jeffries for surliness and bull-headedness."

Ryan wasn't through talking about the fight. Three days before July 4, he told reporters that if the fight took place, he would not be surprised to hear that Flynn lost on a foul. "When Flynn sees that he cannot hit Johnson," Ryan went on, "he will do anything he can in the first place." In the boxing world, such words overtly suggest dirty fighting.

Could there be anything worse in Las Vegas than learning of Ryan's decision to quit? Oh, yes. The day of Ryan's rant turned out to be the same day that Governor William McDonald dropped his own bombshell. McDonald announced he would do everything he could to prevent the Johnson-Flynn fight from taking place.

The parting in May of Ryan and Flynn carried with it an odd postscript, though no more peculiar than any of numerous incidents linked to the championship proceedings. Not long after Ryan and his wife moved into a rented cottage on Grand Avenue in Las Vegas, Ryan decided the place needed some color. He spent eight cents on a clutch of pansies, which he used to decorate the front yard. When he planted the flowers, the world seemed beautiful and bright. Then, almost as quickly as that piece of gardening, Ryan delivered his "hog fat" message, which traveled far and wide.

The backlash from those two words made Ryan realize he had had enough of Las Vegas. He would take Morrow to El Paso for a match and then go on to Juarez for another. Morrow didn't turn many heads in either of those two bouts. He drew both of the fights. It was no surprise that Morrow wound up having an undistinguished boxing career.

Before Ryan left town, he made up his mind that he was not going to give Las Vegas the continued satisfaction of gazing at the pansies—his pansies!— in front of his house. One evening a few days before leaving town, Ryan stopped in front of the Grand Avenue rental house.[9]

Following almost two weeks of intermittent rain, all the pansies were now in glorious full bloom.

Ryan dug up every one of them.

CHAPTER 12

Getting the Old Ring-Around

IF EXCESS BODY flesh created a firestorm nationwide, arguments over the measurements of the boxing ring in Las Vegas brought on a controversy all of its own.

The dimensions of the Las Vegas boxing arena—in this particular case, just the ring—were pored over, argued about, openly criticized, and recalculated again and again. All of this done as if these were specs for a planned adjustment of Rome's Colosseum.

Before the arena went up, Curley and Charles O'Malley looked around Las Vegas for an appropriate site. They finally settled upon a vacant lot at the corner of Sixth Street and Friedman Avenue.

The land sat at the far northern end of the city, approximately a fifteen- to twenty-minute walk from downtown and the railroad station.[1] From the city's high-end neighborhoods on Seventh and Eighth Streets, it would be an even shorter distance. "Good sidewalks can be used all the way," the *Albuquerque Morning Journal* enthused. The site was in plain view of the Santa Fe tracks.

Thus, every passenger who passed through on a daytime train would get a glimpse of the arena. Curley was said to have such a strong lease on the property that nothing short of an injunction would cause him to let go of it. On May 13, a tender by Baker and Lockwood Manufacturing of Kansas City was awarded the job.[2] Baker and Lockwood was primarily a maker and installer of canvas tents for circuses, which seemed appropriate for the clownish doings that had already begun to engulf Las Vegas.

The Kansas City outfit brought in a number of carpenters to erect that structure. Work began June 4. The arena would be portable, and Curley paid the Kansas City firm "in the neighborhood of $5,000 for a one-day rental."

Without realizing it, Curley had permitted use of the arena for more than one day. This was, to be sure, another example of his careless stewardship. The night before the Johnson and Flynn fight, Stanley Yoakum and Rudy Unholz were scheduled to box a twenty-rounder in Las Vegas. That decision would ultimately cost Curley a goodly sum.

Early on, Curley said matters pertaining to the arena were completely out of his hands. The fact is, those matters should have been completely in his hands. Thus, headaches pounded.

With that, the exaggerating began in earnest. Curley and O'Malley predicted an "immense" crowd. Curley clearly was dreaming of another Reno turnout, which drew twenty thousand–plus spectators in an outdoor enclosure that was filled to the brim. Curley doubtless believed that his arena would better that crowd.

On May 20, a Baker and Lockwood representative came to the office of the *Las Vegas Optic* and showed the newspaper's editor a blueprint. There would be a double row of press seats around the ring and a number of VIP box seats. All of this caused the editor of the *Optic* to gush, "There are magnificent views from everywhere." Not quite everywhere. All seats would be at the same level. That said, the view for many would be directly behind a man or woman wearing a hat. Which meant almost everyone in attendance.

The *Optic* found that the least expensive seats in the arena would only be ninety feet from the ring. The structure would be enclosed by a barbed-wire fence and inside there would be canvas walls, each twelve feet high.

Strangely, the structure had just one entrance. If twenty thousand people attempted to get through a single door, a massive logjam would surely occur. Just as worrisome, the top of the arena was to be completely open. If it rained on July the Fourth, a contingency plan did not exist.

Laughable ideas by Curley came almost daily. On May 15, the promoter said there would be no general-admission tickets available. Every one of the 17,950 seats, he explained, was reserved in case the demand for seats was greater than expected, which he assumed would happen. Therefore, someone could buy a ten-dollar ticket, the least expensive, only when the entire place sold out.

Curley apparently clung tightly to the idea that if you built something that was big and new, it would wind up being packed to capacity, no matter the cost.

At the center of the arena stood the ring, which by itself generated a slew of disputes.

Tom Flanagan—Johnson's manager and the supervisor of his training camp, jobs that he had held in Reno—arrived in Las Vegas on June 21. After breakfast that day at the Johnson residence in Old Town, Flanagan strolled out to the site of the arena. En route to New Mexico, Flanagan had read in the newspapers that the ring for the July the Fourth contest measured seventeen and a half feet on all sides.

"The ring looks plenty big enough to me," Flanagan said as he stared at the completed platform.[3]

Johnson, however, wanted it to be bigger—twenty-four feet on all sides. On June 26, Johnson and Curley went to inspect the arena. Johnson did not like what he saw. He insisted the ring be twenty feet inside the ropes. This meant the ring posts would have be removed and the platform widened, among other changes. Curley argued against this. "Jack," he said, "you have fought in smaller rings before and I don't understand why you don't want to do so now."

"No sir," said Johnson. "I fought Jeffries and Tommy Burns in regulation rings."

A tape measure was suddenly produced. The tape indicated that the ring could be expanded to twenty-two feet.

Flynn by now had appeared and he immediately balked at the expansion. He was, however, finally convinced, after much persuasion. Clearly, Curley was trying to give Flynn an edge. The size of the ring would be enlarged.

A week before the fight, the camps of both fighters as well as some newsmen, returned to the arena to check out the ring. Otto Floto, the corpulent columnist for the *Denver Post*, said a smaller ring would not be an impediment for Johnson.[4]

"Jack is always more or less under the impression that someone is putting something over on him," Floto said. "He has in the past been given the worst of it on many occasions. All of Johnson's best fights have been in close quarters. His greatest victories have been won when he and his opponents have been within embracing distances."[5]

Harry Smith of the *San Francisco Chronicle* likely chuckled when he wrote of this summit gathering. "A week ago Johnson didn't care how small the ring was." This new announcement that the ring had to be enlarged was a follow-up for the sake of giving the fight as much publicity as possible.

"It certainly cannot make much difference to Johnson whether the ring is twenty-four feet or seventeen feet," Smith said.[6]

While the ring flap was going on, there came a new jolt. The architectural firm that had designed the arena brought suit against Curley and Las Vegas for the cost of the blueprint. Garnishment action was taken under the lawsuit. Curley responded that he had paid cash to the contractors and all had given their word that the arena would be completed in time.

Meanwhile, squabbling over the size of the ring continued. Johnson's two chief handlers, Tom Flanagan and Watson Burns, along with Curley and Ed Smith, and several sporting editors, motored out to the arena on the morning of June 27.[7]

Flanagan, who earlier had found nothing wrong with the seventeen-foot ring, now said the ring would have to be twenty feet or there would be no fight. After a good deal of haggling, it was decided that the ring would be increased to twenty feet and two inches. Curley said the changes would be too hard to make. After figuring a while, it was found that the ring could be increased to twenty feet, short two inches.

This size was finally accepted by Flanagan and Burns. A bigger ring, the Johnson crew knew, weakened Flynn's chances because Johnson would have more opportunities in a bigger ring where he could chase down Flynn.

Such drawn-out quarreling amused the press. Sporting writers knew it probably did make a difference whether the ring was twenty-four feet or seventeen feet.

The tenth Marquess of Queensbury was a foppish Scot nobleman who, in the middle of the nineteenth century, lent his name to the code of modern boxing. He said rings ought to be twenty-four feet on all four sides. So much for that storied gent's bestowment.

By the end of all the quibbling, it was clear that Johnson and Flynn didn't really care all that much about the size of the ring.

"I can whip Johnson inside a barrel," bragged Flynn.

"I can whip Flynn in a ring the width of an electric wire," Johnson gloated.

It is doubtful that anyone within earshot paid attention to either fighter's bombast. This much was true: reporters were certain that Johnson would win the size-of-the-ring altercation.

As one sporting writer put it, "Whoever heard of a champion losing an argument?"

CHAPTER 13

Here Come the Cars

IF THE PRIZEFIGHT ring was ready, so were the many automobiles that had started to show up in Las Vegas.

During the days and weeks before the fight, journalists, spectators, and the curious journeyed to New Mexico by all manner of transportation: railroad (including boxcars), automobile, horseback, burro, and in one case, a motorcycle. A grizzled prospector arrived with a dog team.[1]

By far the majority of those making the journey did so by passenger train. Train travel's popularity was due to its swiftness and all-around comfort. Federal Highway Administration records indicate that the automobile was still something of an unusual sight in 1912. Not everyone had a "machine," as they were then known.

There were only 901,400 motor vehicles in the US registered that year.[2] It is difficult to track how many licenses existed at the time, for some states issued such documents, while many more did not.

Jack Johnson, his wife, chauffeur, and sparring partners had a Santa Fe Railroad car almost to themselves when they left Chicago for New Mexico. On June 3, aboard another train, Johnson's Chalmers Detroit 40—his roomy, open-topped touring car—arrived at the Las Vegas depot.

The Chalmers had room for seven people. When filled to capacity, the machine resembled a convertible bus. The auto was upholstered in hand-buffed leather, finished in the costliest way. Johnson had paid $2,750 for the vehicle. Johnson also had a French 120-horsepower racing car, which he drove at breakneck speeds, skidded for the fun of it, and barreled along in full of overconfidence and indifference.

Those who owned automobiles in 1912 were not motorists. They were "autoists."³ Autoists were an elite lot. They often belonged to special clubs, much like today's car collectors who congregate in various cities to inspect, say, each other's Ford Thunderbird.

Johnson was a familiar sight in Las Vegas, for he motored regularly in the city. When he got behind wheel of his massive car, people took note. When he bought by mail order a vulcanizer, a device that mended the rubber in automobile tires, the simple act made news in the *Las Vegas Optic*.⁴ Johnson said no car was complete without a vulcanizer.

For the most part, residents were fascinated when they saw Johnson driving about. Owning a car of any kind was still relatively new to the community. Reporters who came in the afternoons to see Johnson train in his yard were frequently disappointed. Where was the champion? Johnson liked to take afternoon drives, typically in the company of his wife and a sparring partner or two, plus his chauffeur, Charles Brown.

On one of his auto jaunts, Johnson headed out to Mora, New Mexico, a village about thirty miles away, mostly on a bad road. When he arrived there, a small band of musicians welcomed him.

Itching to go fishing one mid-June afternoon, Johnson traveled twenty miles to the north. His favorite destination was a region called Ten Lakes, near the village of Watrous, New Mexico. When Johnson had fished enough, the group in the Chalmers began to make its way back toward Las Vegas. It wasn't long before a Santa Fe Railroad express train roared by them. Johnson, who didn't mind being a passenger in his vehicle, this time climbed over the seat and grabbed the wheel from his chauffeur.

The race was on.⁵

Inside of a mile, Johnson managed to pull even with the passenger train. There were four people with Johnson in the big Chalmers. Five black men in all, plus Etta, so very pale she covered up nearly completely in the strong sunshine.

One can only imagine the looks given those in the Chalmers by the passengers on the train. The travelers in the large auto frantically held tightly to the seats as the touring car bumped and rattled alongside the railroad tracks at forty-five miles per hour.

Johnson, who never turned down any sort of competition, constantly flashed his wide, glowing smile at the train as it and he flew south, side by side.⁶

A mile north of Las Vegas, with Johnson's car now fading to the midpoint of the train, the road split off from the tracks. When the train disappeared from sight, the challenge ended.

The engineer and passengers on the train spread the word about the race. Johnson, however, was silent when he returned to his camp. This was not because the train had nosed out his automobile. Rather, he had promised Jack Curley that he would not take risks of such kind until after July the Fourth.

Several newspapermen got wind of the incident and, alarming as the performance was, they poked fun at it. Going fast behind the wheel seemed to be in Johnson's blood. On April 14, before he came to Las Vegas, Johnson was arrested for speeding in Evanston, Illinois, while motoring with Etta. When he appeared before the justice of the peace, he realized he did not have one cent in his possession. The justice smiled and said, "That's all right, Jack. I'll trust you until Thursday when your court hearing comes up."

Speeding was Johnson's adrenalin. He had been arrested for breaking the speed limit on two occasions in San Francisco, one of those just before he left for Reno to fight Jeffries. The second violation cost him twenty days in jail.

A tale of Johnson's fast driving was repeated often over the years until it became legend.

Tearing along a highway toward some unnamed town, he was stopped by a policeman. The fine, the cop who pulled him over said, would be ten dollars. Johnson handed the officer twenty dollars. The policeman looked puzzled. Said Johnson, "In a couple of days, I'll be coming back this way."

Not everyone was taken with Johnson's yen for lickety-split driving. In his column in the *Evening World*, a New York City newspaper, Robert Edgren wrote, "Johnson has a propensity for road burning.[7] He ran into the law in London when he was fighting there."

Edgren wondered in print how much money Johnson had given to lawyers and paid out in fines. "His troubles have been caused more by sheer carelessness and irresponsibility than by wickedness."

Edgren continued: "Still, it will be a good thing for the sport of boxing when we have a heavyweight champion who figures more in the ring reports and less in the police news."

Johnson drove his car whenever he felt like it; skittering along in a fast automobile was his way to relax. Speed-limit signs? They were put there for everyone to see but Johnson.

Johnson's auto accident on April 24, near Pittsburgh, nearly caused the fight to be called off. Johnson's car had been hit by a large truck. It's probable that Johnson exaggerated the injuries he cited. He said he could not raise his right arm. His right shoulder, his spine, and the muscles of the right side of his back left him in pain. Johnson blamed his own driver as well as the truck driver. His car was destroyed and he filed suit against the truck driver.

"If I had been driving the automobile, the accident never would have happened," Johnson told reporter Walter Eckersall of the *Chicago Tribune*.[8]

Automobile accidents were frequent in 1912. After all, many autoists had never taken lessons or been told how to drive safely. Deaths on the roads were a common occurrence. That year saw 2,968 motoring fatalities in a country with 95 million people.

Las Vegas was not immune to automobile mishaps. J. E. Speare, a Santa Fe Railroad foreman wound up in the Railway Hospital at Las Vegas for serious injuries received when an automobile driven by William Adlon of Las Vegas struck the railroader's vehicle. Speare said he did not see or hear the machine until it was too late to avoid. Adlon said he was not traveling fast.[9]

Jack Curley's wife was not traveling fast either when, to avoid a collision with a Las Vegas streetcar, she steered her machine into a telephone pole at the corner of Plaza and Pacific Streets.[10]

Two of boxing's best-known sporting writers had challenges not with the Johnson-Flynn fight, but with a four-wheel machine. Sandy Griswold, sporting editor of the *Omaha World-Herald*, and Bob Edgren were on their way to Las Vegas on June 28, along with Omaha sporting enthusiast F. C. Hurley who was their chauffeur.[11]

Very near Brighton, Colorado, the driver dozed and failed to make a turn in the road. The car, a Valle, almost as well-equipped as a Pullman coach, plunged into Stanley Lake and sank in fifteen feet of water. The four men swam safely to shore, while the car remained at the bottom of the lake. The men walked to Denver, a distance of nineteen miles. They wore neither hats, coats, nor shoes when they arrived at a local hotel. Most of their clothes had disappeared with the submerged automobile.

Another sporting editor met with trouble while driving, this time in Las Vegas, New Mexico. On the afternoon of the fight, the *Denver Post's* Otto Floto was obliged to run his automobile up on a Las Vegas sidewalk in order to avoid a collision with a horse and buggy. Floto was arrested but released when he was found not guilty of careless driving.

By 1912, most large cities had decent roads. Some were even paved. Beyond major cities was a different story. In rural sections, roads were little more than dirt trails that could turn to mud-packed passages overnight.

H. W. Lanigan wrote that the roads between Las Vegas and Denver would be in excellent shape by the first of July. Many tourists from the capital of Colorado had made plans to come in automobiles to witness the Johnson-Flynn bout.

Some of those tourists almost didn't make it.[12] J. F. Gunthorpe of Denver, traveling in a big touring car, and accompanied by William W. Arnett, a former deputy sheriff of Denver and a good friend of Curley's, got stuck while attempting to ford some water just north of Watrous, New Mexico. Gunthorpe hired the owner of a team of horses to pull his automobile out of the water and the mud, which was said to be as easy to maneuver in as a field of molasses.

Surely the moral to the many automobile woes was this: When in doubt, take the train.

CHAPTER 14

All Aboard!

IF YOU BELIEVED newspaper accounts of the number of people making their way to Las Vegas in mid-1912, you might think half the country intended to be there. H. W. Lanigan, the tireless press agent for the championship, definitely had a hand in dispensing such information. Starting in May, Lanigan wrote articles in the offices of Albuquerque's two daily newspapers. By mid-June he had stationed himself at the *Las Vegas Optic*.[1]

Presumably he could have better access in Las Vegas to the fighters and to Curley for information that clearly stretched the facts. These were stories in which Lanigan excelled. Lanigan continued to send his work to Albuquerque newspapers, as well to the *Santa Fe New Mexican* and even to newspapers out of the state.

The expected enormous crowds that would be coming to see the fight was the type of news Lanigan generated almost daily. The *Optic* had a tiny staff. The editor and publisher, M. M. Padgett, apparently was happy to have someone of Lanigan's writing acumen turn out as much copy as he wished. The reports of fans traveling to Las Vegas began to filter in soon after Memorial Day. Such plans almost entirely involved passenger trains.

According to Lanigan, Curley was certain of a capacity crowd from the states of New Mexico, Arizona, West Texas (not quite a state), Oklahoma, Kansas, Missouri, and Colorado. John O. Talbott, a well-known Denver financier, announced his plan to order ten Pullman trains to Las Vegas.[2]

Talbott had formerly worked in the circus business. That fact alone would likely have made him feel at home in the spectacle growing in Las Vegas. Many trains were said to be coming from towns in New Mexico. For instance, a special train in Clovis would be hooking up two Pullman cars. One hundred and fifty people were expected in the Clovis Special; many fans it was believed would be from Clovis, Melrose, Roswell, and Amarillo.[3]

The *Chicago Tribune* reported that a train from Terre Haute indicated that at least two hundred fans would be coming to the fight by special trains from that town and from Indianapolis. Positive news such as this was kept up, even as Governor William McDonald's interference cloud remained overhead. Simply, Curley oozed confidence and Lanigan took his cues from Curley.

On May 17, the promoter told the *Albuquerque Morning Journal* that orders for seats continued to pour in and he was sure that the seating capacity of 17,950 would be met.

Nearly seventy-five people, including a number of women, left Santa Fe on July 3 for Las Vegas, reported the *Santa Fe New Mexican*. Seven automobiles, averaging five people to each machine, made the trip. The Santa Fe travelers took with them camping equipment and well-stocked food boxes.

Rather than stay in Las Vegas to see the fight, several of the Santa Fe arrivals planned to return to Santa Fe to boost the De Vargas Day celebration on July 5. It is likely that Curley did not understand who De Vargas was or why he mattered.

From Baltimore came word to Curley on May 31 that a large number of fight followers would be coming to Las Vegas and would sit at ringside. Lanigan reported that W. A. Stewart, an oilman from Tulsa, Oklahoma, would be there with many of his pals.[4] More than five hundred people from Denver would be crowding into special fight trains, according to Lanigan on June 9. The reservations were coming in so fast that the trains would be filled. Those waiting to go by train, Lanigan wrote, would do well to make their reservations at once. An extra Pullman would be attached to the special at Colorado Springs, which would be packed with fight lovers from that city.

On June 8, a special train with twelve cars carried 250 members of the Knights and Ladies of Security, representing councils in the Midwest, stopped in Las Vegas.

While the train waited at the station, Charles O'Malley, nearly as busy as Lanigan in touting the fight, went through the passenger cars handing out cartoon postcards of Las Vegas, which the travelers "gobbled up like hotcakes."

Many of those aboard went into town to have dinner before the train left. Somewhere the tourists got the idea that Johnson and Flynn would both be at the station when the special arrived. Such travelers were disappointed when they learned that the two pugilists were not around but were training in their respective camps. There were plans made for those travelers to come to the fight on their return trip.

W. D. Scoville, a well-known boxing and wrestling promoter from Kansas City, telegraphed that he would be bringing a trainload of fight fans from that city. Scoville apparently made arrangements for a round-trip rate of $21.50 between Kansas City and Las Vegas. All the seats on that train were taken almost as soon as the news got out. Scoville said the residents of Kansas City were "going batty" over the Johnson-Flynn engagement. "Those people would fill a great many seats," Lanigan declared.

Once the travelers arrived in Las Vegas, the hunt began for a place to stay. By June 26, rooms at all hotels were nearly booked. In fact, the town looked more and more like a tent city. Shelters of all sizes were popping up here and there, often in vacant tracts. The National Guard Armory, the Opera House, and the Commercial Club's rooms had been fixed up as dormitories. Residents put signs on their porches or in their front yards advertising that cots were available within. More than one hundred passengers engaged berths on a special train from Pueblo.

That train supposedly was the "most magnificent ever run on an occasion of this kind." The fare had been placed so low that the trip was made available to almost any fan who cared to go. All those coming from any part of Colorado would be taken on this train. Ladies would be admitted to any and all seats at ringside.

Prices ranged from sixteen dollars to twenty dollars per person, depending on whether it was a lower or upper berth.

The Pueblo fans, almost all of them friends of Flynn, it seemed, wore large white hats with the words "Pueblo Colorado" on them.

According to the *Pueblo Chieftain* newspaper, those fans were going to Las Vegas with pockets full of money to back their enthusiasm for Flynn as "the greatest white man of them all."[5]

Surely the most unconventional group of travelers, it was reported, would be heading to Las Vegas from tiny Obar, New Mexico.[6] They would not be going by train but by horseback. A communiqué had been received at the Flynn headquarters that one hundred cowboys, led by Bill Banner, would ride into Las Vegas on saddles. The distance between the two places, if you go by today's highway system, is 166 miles. By horseback in 1912, the distance would have been approximately 110 miles, most of it over hilly rangeland.

The Obar ranch a century ago was owned by Battling Nelson, the celebrated lightweight fighter who was offbeat in his own right. Born Oscar Mathaeus Nielsen in Denmark, Nelson grew up in Chicago. In neither place did a large number of cowboys call it home.

Obar sits in a sparsely populated spot of Quay County, eight miles southwest of Nara Visa, New Mexico.[7] In the early 1900s, the community sprang up on the north side of the Chicago, Rock Island, and Pacific railroad tracks. At that time, the settlement was called Perry, for a local man. The name was eventually changed to Obar. That happened because the Circle Bar Ranch's brand was a circle with a bar beneath it.

At one point, the New Mexico Land and Immigration Company promoted the community heavily. One newspaper advertisement foresaw Obar as a boomtown. "Keep Your Eye on Obar" the ad proclaimed. "Nothing can keep Obar down more than it could hold back Chicago, Seattle, Oklahoma City or San Francisco."

At the peak of its prominence, which didn't last long, Obar had approximately two dozen buildings. One abandoned structure is all that remains today.

Bill Banner, it turned out, was an old friend of Curley's. Banner swore he would sell forty to fifty tickets for the fight on the Fourth, just in his town of Obar.

Perhaps the wildest promise of attendance at the fight came from the *Albuquerque Evening Herald* and very likely from the swift fingers of H. W. Lanigan. On page 1 of that newspaper for June 4 was the incredulous headline: "Thousand Negroes Plan to Descend on Meadow City."

Could this be so? One thousand? Various photographs of fans inside the arena on July the Fourth show few black spectators. Where then did this hard-to-believe statistic come from? It was not stated in the story, but this subheadline provided the following: "Dusky followers of champion travel to Las Vegas in special train from Oklahoma and Denver."

FIGURE 1. Jack Johnson grins at the Las Vegas crowd during the 1912 prizefight, which he did numerous times. Meanwhile, Jim Flynn holds on to the champion in preparation to head-butt Johnson, an illegal maneuver that the challenger attempted often in the bout. (Photo courtesy of Annie Leonard.)

FIGURE 2. Jim Flynn shadowboxes at his Las Vegas training camp located near the Montezuma Castle. Shadowboxing was a training method Flynn did frequently during the run-up to the world heavyweight championship battle. (Photo courtesy of the George Grantham Bain Collection, Library of Congress.)

FIGURE 3. The Las Vegas, New Mexico, house where Jack Johnson lived with his wife and where he trained. A boxing ring and bleachers were set up in Johnson's yard for fans to sit and watch the champion's workouts. Spectators were charged to view those workouts. The house, just off the plaza, still stands. (Photo courtesy of the Gilberto Espinosa Collection. Image is owned by Margaret Espinosa McDonald.)

FIGURE 4. Holding his coat and hat, Jim Flynn arrives in Las Vegas on May 9 to a
large, mostly male crowd and a brass band at the railroad station. The slender man
in the bowler hat to Flynn's right is Charles F. O'Malley, one of three local businessmen who helped to bring a world championship to New Mexico. (Photo courtesy of
Annie Leonard.)

FIGURE 5. Jack Johnson arrives at the Las Vegas, New Mexico, railroad station,
along with his wife, Etta Terry Duryea, on May 28. A sizable brass band also met the
couple. (Photo courtesy of the City of Las Vegas Museum, New Mexico.)

FIGURE 6. The construction of a prizefight arena at the northern end of Las Vegas, New Mexico, took more than three weeks. There were 17,500 wooden seats available when the structure was completed. However, only 3,000–4,500 fans showed up to buy tickets. (Photo courtesy of the City of Las Vegas Museum, New Mexico.)

FIGURE 7. William C. McDonald, the governor of the new state of New Mexico, did not like the idea of a fight between a white man and a black man. For five months McDonald refused to let the bout go on. A few days before the contest McDonald gave in and decided the fight could proceed. (Photo courtesy of the Palace of the Governors Photo Archives, Santa Fe. Negative no. 047795.)

FIGURE 8. Jack Johnson and his wife take a break on the porch of the house the couple rented on Gonzales Street, just off the plaza. Both became familiar figures around Las Vegas. (Photo courtesy of the City of Las Vegas Museum, New Mexico.)

FIGURE 9. Jack Johnson sits in the back seat of his large automobile. Those with him are sparring partners and various pals. All are getting ready to motor around nearby roads. Johnson drove often on these short trips because it was a chance for him to get away from the hubbub of Las Vegas and see the countryside. Now and then he would let one of his camp do the driving. (Photo courtesy of the Palace of the Governors Photo Archives, Santa Fe. Negative no. 087475.)

FIGURE 10. In mid-May, Curley hired Tommy Ryan, a veteran trainer and a clever fighter in his days as a middleweight. Curley believed that Ryan would help get Flynn in shape before he faced Johnson. Sporting writers and boxing fans saluted this move. Everything was going along fine in Flynn's camp when the word got out that Flynn and Ryan were not getting along. Their bickering turned to foul words. Ryan decided he had had enough and departed Las Vegas. (Photo courtesy of the George Grantham Bain Collection, Library of Congress.)

FIGURE 11. Johnson frequently worked out solo in Las Vegas, often going shirtless. The champion was proud of his physique and often posed that way for visitors. Now and then he would wear a bathrobe outside on the grounds of his camp. (Photo courtesy of the Palace of the Governors Photo Archives, Santa Fe. Jesse Nusbaum Collection. Negative no. 061303.)

FIGURE 12. Johnson typically had a smile on his face, even during arduous training sessions. He obviously knew that the upcoming fight was clearly his to win. He smiled also because fans would have to pay fifteen cents to watch the workouts in his back-yard. (Photo courtesy of the George Grantham Bain Collection, Library of Congress.)

FIGURE 13. At 2:45 p.m., the two fighters; the referee, Ed Smith; and various seconds gathered in the ring of the arena to discuss issues that might come up during the fight. No hitting below the belt, no head-butting, no holding. (Photo courtesy of the George Grantham Bain Collection, Library of Congress.)

FIGURE 14. Because there were no radio broadcasts in 1912, fight fans gathered in front of various newspaper offices across the country. The *Star-Journal* in Pueblo, Colorado, was no exception. As in many similar places in the country, spectators stood outside while those inside used megaphones to tell fans how the fight was going, who was winning, and who was not doing very well. (Photo courtesy of the Rawlins Public Library Special Collections, Pueblo, Colorado.)

FIGURE 15. Captain Fred Fornoff of the New Mexico Mounted Police, who was easily identified by a ten-gallon hat that he wore, climbed into the ring shortly after the ninth round began. Fornoff announced that the fight was over, he said, because Governor McDonald had told him to do so. Spectators and newsmen booed loudly at such a decision. (Photo of Fornoff courtesy of Chuck Hornung.)

FIGURE 16. Meanwhile, chaos reigned. Fans squeezed into the ring looking for answers but finding nothing. The world heavyweight championship continued to belong to a black man. (Photo courtesy of Chris Cozzone.)

LAS VEGAS 'BATTLE' WORST IN HISTORY OF AMERICAN RING

Flynn, Outclassed in Every Way, Fails Even to Live Up to His Reputation as a Gamester, Using Foul Tactics During Contest.

AFFAIR A TERRIBLE "KNOCK" TO THE ONCE SPLENDID SPORT

FIGURES 17A and 17b. Newspapers the following day did not have kind words in their headlines or illustrations. Everyone who saw the fight or read about it surely felt disgusted. Chicago's *Inter Ocean* called the match "The Worst in the History of the American Ring."

CHAPTER 15

He's Got Mail

ON FEBRUARY 8, Governor William C. McDonald announced that he was against the prizefight and hoped the state legislature would pass an anti-fight law.[1] McDonald said that he would use mounted police if necessary to enforce such a law and prevent the contest from happening.

In fact, McDonald went on to say that he did not care for the prizefight in Las Vegas or anywhere in New Mexico. Mostly McDonald worried about what the event would bring along with it. That meant such shady characters as bunco artists, hucksters, pikers, pettifoggers, thieves, and every sort of chiseler under the sun.

The governor also wanted a bill to outlaw prizefighting altogether in the newly recognized state, something he could never make happen. Even so he hung on to his beliefs.

Why exactly did McDonald make such an edict? He held nothing personal against Las Vegas as a place. In fact, he had been married in that city on August 31, 1891. His wife, the former Francis McCourt, was a widow with four small children. He surely held a soft spot in his heart for Las Vegas, or Meadow City, as many referred to it.

Ironically, word spread that McDonald had boxed in his younger days. However, no one seemed to know where or when he put on the gloves. This much is known and was reported: The governor did not wish to be understood as being opposed to boxing matches of the "clean and manly kind." But he was bitterly opposed to boxing matches, especially those between white men and black men.

Why then did he have reservations about the fight? McDonald grew up in a religious environment. He attended a seminary in upstate New York and that could have set him against all manner of pugilism. In response to his February announcement, the governor received dozens and dozens of letters. These came not just from New Mexico residents but from people far and wide.

The letters sent to McDonald ranged from the all-in-favor-of-not-having-the-contest to a very few who thought the fight ought to go on as scheduled.[2] To nearly all the letter writers, the governor's secretary, C. H. Olsen, sent this form reply: "The governor has made no statement concerning the prizefight other than to reiterate what he stated when the fight was first talked of last spring."

On June 17, A. L. Murphy, the publisher of the *San Francisco Examiner*, mailed this message to McDonald: "What are your intentions about the fight? It would be to the *Examiner*'s advantage to know, as it will save the paper the expense of sending its Sporting Editor to the fight."

On June 19, Olsen responded, as he did to many, many other letter writers.

A single letter that McDonald personally replied to was delivered to R. L. Jones of Cimarron, New Mexico, on June 9, 1912: "I have received a letter dated June 6th with your name signed to it by some other person stating that a canvass of your town shows there are 317 who are in favor of the Johnson-Flynn fight on July 4 and only seven against. If that is a fact that Cimarron is almost unanimous for that sort of exhibition, I can only say that I am sorry it is so."

The vast majority of letters opposing the fight came from religious-affiliated organizations, in New Mexico as well as other states.[3] On February 12, only days after McDonald's proclamation, William J. Downing, the secretary of the Pastors' Conference, composed of all Protestant ministers in Las Cruces, wrote this: "By unanimous vote at this regular meeting I want to express to you their hearty approval of your action in refusing to permit prizefighting in this state."

Arthur Tillman, president of the First Christian Church of Las Vegas, wrote on February 12, 1912, "We profoundly believe that prizefighting and its attendant evils are extremely detrimental to the best material, social, educational and spiritual interests of our state."

From many states, the Christian Endeavor Union led the charge condemning the fight. The following was dated April 27, 1912, and it came from the president of the Tennessee Christian Endeavor Union:

I have just learned with much regret that New Mexico expects to cele-brate her first Fourth of July with a prizefight between a negro and a white man, to be held in Las Vegas. I wish I had the power and wisdom to convince you that your great State must not afford to begin her career by countenancing such an affair. In the name of decency and manhood; in the name of the Great Father of the Universe, I beg and plead with you to do everything in your power to prevent this fight.

Very sincerely yours, Eugene Philpot

Not every letter railed against the fight.[4] C. L. Carter, chief land sur-veyor for Roosevelt County and a resident of Portales, New Mexico, wrote on June 7, 1912: "I think it is a shame for a white man to fight a negro that way. Born in Virginia, raised in the South, the youngest of six brothers in the Confederate Army, I am a true friend of the negro. I feel the negro problem is harder to solve now than in 1860. May God direct your steps."

The Laguna Indians also took issue with the fight.[5] The tribe sent a war chief to protest the matter with McDonald. A war chief did not care for box-ing? That seemed so, apparently. The Pueblo Indians shouted unsuccessfully for immediate antiprizefight legislation in the brand-new, forty-seventh state, instead of engaging in what was termed "a disgraceful sort of business."[6]

Pastors in Clovis, New Mexico, were dead set in their protest of future boxing matches in that city. Women's groups in Clovis felt the same way. Much of these feelings came not just because of the Flynn-Johnson fight on the state's horizon, but because of a recent and savage prizefight held at Clo-vis's Lyceum Club between Everett Winters of Raton and Benny Pappan, a part Native American from Oklahoma.

Women's groups in Clovis, in particular the Women's Christian Temper-ance Union, decided to take a stand. They spoke up by announcing how much they thoroughly detested the idea of a prizefight in their fair city.

However, several businessmen in Clovis firmly held their ground. In fact, the men met to discuss whether there was sufficient sentiment and cash to warrant purchasing a large assembly tent from a Kansas City, Missouri, firm. That tent would be used for prizefights. Such a tent would help Clovis become a true boxing center, which eventually did happen.[7]

CHAPTER 16

Rolling Out the Stereotypes

IN 1912, WHEREVER there were black people in New Mexico, racial incidents seemed to follow. And yet racism was not a dominant force in the state. The 1910 census reveals that out of a total population of 327,301, only 1,628 or 0.5 percent were classified as black.

There is no clear evidence that Johnson's presence in the brand-new state elevated bigotry by itself.[1] Nonetheless, his arrival did cause white people to look at African Americans differently.

This curious news item about Johnson appeared June 6 in the *Las Vegas Optic*: "When he (Johnson) spent eight dollars for four large watermelons, which were imported from Florida for his especial delectation, Jack Johnson displayed one of the characteristics of his race."

Therefore, when Johnson learned that Ike Davis, owner of the Cash Grocer in Las Vegas, had received four melons directly from Florida, "Johnson cheerfully forked up two dollars each for the toothsome dainties, which weigh altogether 120 pounds."

The *Las Vegas Optic* was surely one of the worst newspapers in terms of using language that today would be entirely inappropriate. Johnson's mother and sister came to Las Vegas for a couple of days. "They were to be in charge of the culinary department and see that Johnson's table is supplied with the best of eatables, prepared as only a southern mammy can cook them."

The hue of someone's color did matter in Las Vegas.[2] The organizers of the Johnson-Flynn fight made sure there were black pennants and white pennants for sale at the arena, and encouraged fans to wave the pennant of the same hue as the man for whom they rooted. Suffice it to say that many more white souvenirs than black were sold and would be waved about the arena during the match.

That sort of treatment didn't much bother Johnson. He was the nightmare that woke white supremacists in a cold sweat. He was simply big, black, and belligerent. If others were irked by his actions, that was not his problem.

Was Jack Curley prejudiced? It's highly doubtful, for he gave much more attention to money matters than he did to skin color. Even so, Curley ordered advertising flyers for newspapers to use on fight day. Beneath a large photograph of Flynn was this announcement: "Jim Flynn, of Pueblo Colorado, best of the White Men."

Flynn certainly showed racist tendencies. He dropped the N-word on Johnson in the ring and out of it. He referred to Mexican Americans as "greasers." His language bothered so many people in New Mexico that the *Santa Fe New Mexican* made mention of it.[3]

Sports writers who covered the fight thought nothing of inserting racist remarks in their stories. One of the most apt to do this was C. W. Patrick, sporting editor of the *Pueblo Star-Journal*. A rock-solid Flynn supporter and boundless admirer of the Puebloan, Patrick wrote in his July the Fourth column, "It is not flattering to have the championship rest outside the Caucasian race. Flynn is going to bring the championship back where it belongs. Whether you admire Flynn or not, whether you believe in his ability or not, you must shake hands with him on this score. Not through any malice or cheap hatred at all, but merely for the pride of race, we all wish Jim Flynn success."[4]

One of Johnson's Las Vegas sparring partners was Calvin Respress. John Day, a sporting writer from Chicago, wrote this of Respress. "He is better known as 'Rastus' in these parts. He is a tar baby bull and looks like some missing link."[5]

Beginning in circa 1890, Rastus was the Cream of Wheat chef. His opposite from that same period was Aunt Jemima, celebrated queen of breakfast items. Today, both names are pejorative terms and are considered offensive.

Similarly, editorial cartoons in many newspapers in 1912 could not resist depicting Johnson as monkey-like. That typically meant huge lips, bug eyes, skinny arms and legs, and a grin as wide as an open barn door.

The lone exception to this was a cartoonist/sportswriter named Thomas Aloysius Dorgan, better known as "Tad" from his initials. Dorgan had loved boxing and as a boy wanted to be a fighter until his right hand was crushed in an accident and four fingers were lost. From there on Dorgan drew and wrote with his left hand. Johnson and Dorgan first met in 1901 and soon became very close. Dorgan died in 1929 at age fifty-two. "Tad was the one writer who always asked for a fair deal for me," Johnson said.[6]

Dorgan crossed the cartoon color line, just as Johnson punched his way over one in boxing.

Several reporters who interviewed Johnson seemed to take delight in exaggerating his speech, making him sound like an uneducated bumpkin from cotton fields of the Deep South. A cartoon that appeared in numerous newspapers nationwide featured a drawing of a smiling gorilla-like head and these accompanying words: "Dar's sompin' mighty funny 'bout dese white folks' laws. Dey arrests a guy an' puts 'im in jail fo' fast drivin' in a auto an' dey arrest 'im an' raise a awful row when he buys de'mons in London an' fergits to pay de dooty—but 'Lan's sakes! Dey frames up a scheme fo' dat same guy to beat up a po' lil' white man like misto Flynn fo' a big pot of money, which is sholy like stealin' candy from a baby, an' dey aint no law 'bout dat no how—seems mighty funny, da's all!"[7]

One reporter in Las Vegas likened Johnson's complexion to "the entrance of a busy underground tunnel in Chicago at midnight."[8] Johnson's win over Jeffries enraged white boxing fans who were denied this symbol of a supreme being.

There would never have been a heavyweight championship prizefight in Las Vegas if Johnson hadn't agreed to take part. The city may have welcomed him, but other black men there were not always made to feel at home.

On June 6, a black hobo named John Pennington was arrested on the charge of vagrancy, part of a concerted effort by Las Vegas to "clean up the city" for the prizefight. In Pennington's arraignment on June 7, Judge D. R. Murray sentenced Pennington to thirty days of work on the city chain gang. Six other hobos were arrested that day and after spending the night in the city jail were turned loose with orders to leave town. Pennington was given a similar opportunity but evidently wanted to stick around until the John-son-Flynn bout. Pennington did not gain his freedom until two days after the fight concluded.

Lynchings unfortunately were regular occurrences throughout the United Sates during Johnson's time in Las Vegas, including the day he arrived in the state. In early June of 1912, word came that several Clovis, New Mexico, men and youths fired a number of gunshots at a house in the south part of Clovis where several black families lived.[9]

This action was blamed on people not from Clovis but from elsewhere in eastern New Mexico's Curry County. The rowdy group had come into the town on a Saturday night for some excitement, and then mounted their horses and escaped the scene. Several law-enforcement officers appeared a short time after the incident, but those who fired the shots were not immediately found.

Eventually, a Mr. John Kizer was charged with inciting a riot in Clovis in order to drive black people from the town.[10] A district judge released Kizer, citing no direct evidence against the man. Two days later, Kizer was "re-arrested" for impersonating an officer. Why or how that was accomplished is not clear. Two other men were being held in jail on riot charges and three more were to face charges.[11]

Numerous onlookers packed a preliminary hearing for the men at the Justice of the Peace Court in Clovis. With such a large crowd on hand, the floor of that courtroom gave way and collapsed beneath the enormous weight. No one was hurt seriously.[12]

In late June, a conference of railroad men and local citizens was held in Clovis to discuss the attitude of certain people in the town toward black employees of the Santa Fe Railroad who might in the future come to Clovis to live. The citizens made it plain that the people of Clovis were fully in sympathy with the upholding of the law and for protection of all, regardless of color.

Much regret was expressed about the attention Clovis had received from the acts of five or six irresponsible persons who had since fled the town. Two rewards of $250 each were offered by citizens present. One for the apprehension and conviction of any of those guilty of the recent disturbance among the town's black community, and one for the arrest and conviction of anyone guilty of such conduct in the future.

Presumably, this conference was held on the ground floor.

The alleged riot in Clovis brought forth a great many lawmen, among them three New Mexico mounted policemen. One of those on horseback was Captain Fred Fornoff, who would shortly become a pariah-like, ham-handed figure in the Johnson-Flynn fight.[13]

The *Clovis News* had this to say about the presence of the mounted police: "The intimidating and dominant manner of one of the Santa Fe officers in criticizing the court for not arresting every other man in town came near causing more serious trouble than the Negro problem."[14]

Being the highest ranking of the three mounted policemen, Fornoff surely was the chief intimidator.

Cloudcroft, New Mexico, located in the Sacramento Mountains, was also experiencing racial difficulties. In early June, Governor McDonald received dispatches from Otero County officials that indicated an effort to drive out the black population from that popular resort. The sheriff of Otero County reported that this was merely the work of hoodlums and that he could handle the situation without incident.[15]

CHAPTER 17

Eenie, Meenie, Miney, Moe

THE PROCESS USED in selecting a referee for the Johnson-Flynn contest bore more than a slight resemblance to the well-known counting rhyme—and the explicit racism of its original iteration—employed by children.

On June 10, Jack Curley presented Johnson with a tentative list of thirteen names of referees who, Curley said, were eligible for the job.[1] Curley informed Johnson that Flynn had already seen the list and had gone over it, without saying much. The majority of those men were sporting editors who likely would be coming to New Mexico to report on the fight.[2]

Having a reporter write about a fight he had just judged from inside the ropes seemed difficult at best. But such a thing occurred regularly in 1912, for "newspaper decisions" often were made by the referee, who frequently was a newspaperman.

Curley asked Johnson to give careful consideration to Albuquerque's Mark Levy, who had been around boxing for a good while and had worked tirelessly in preparation for the championship fight during the run-up.[3] As for Charles O'Malley, who chaired the committee that brought the fight to Las Vegas, his refereeing experience, if it existed at all, was minimal. Same for J. Porter Jones, an Albuquerque automobile salesman.

Because he managed Flynn, Curley was of course ruled out as a potential candidate. No one questioned the importance of selecting the best man. Forty-eight hours before the 1910 Johnson-Jeffries fight, differences over who would be the referee could still be heard. At that point, Tex Rickard, who had done most of the promoting of the Reno fight, announced himself as the referee.

Those who had followed from a distance the goings-on of the Fight of the Century considered Rickard unseasoned, unprepared, and unqualified to take that role. For one, Rickard had been a very busy man all the morning of the fight, attending to myriad details. For him, getting in the ring would be akin to having a school kid take the mound and pitch to Ty Cobb.

Such criticism didn't bother Rickard. Chomping on a cigar and wearing a suit and necktie, he confidently stepped through the ropes. How did he do? Rickard managed to keep order as Johnson repeatedly pummeled a stunned Jim Jeffries.

Three times Johnson consigned the illustrious champion to the canvas. The third flooring gave Johnson a TKO pasting in fifteen rounds. Jeffries admitted later that even on his very best days he could not have defeated Johnson.

On June 12, Johnson stopped in at Curley's office on Centre Street and said in no way did he wish to see a New York City gent preside over the fight.

This meant that Johnson did not want Sam Austin, the sporting editor for the *National Police Gazette* and an experienced referee who had overseen fifty-six bouts. Nor did Johnson desire "Honest John" Kelly, a former major-league baseball umpire turned saloonkeeper turned gambling-hall operator, who had recently taken up officiating boxing events.

Further, Johnson was uncomfortable with any New York City arbitrator, and for good reason. Even a liberal newspaper such as the *New York Times* had been openly hostile to the champion, particularly following his victories over Tommy Burns and Jim Jeffries. Moreover, Johnson detested the New York State Boxing Commissioner.[4]

Johnson was pleased when he saw the names of Jack Welch and Ed Smith on the list. And he didn't mind that Mark Levy, an unknown quantity outside New Mexico, was there.[5] "They tell me he is all right," Johnson told a reporter. Both Flynn and Johnson wanted Curley to referee. The promoter vigorously shook his head no.

When Johnson scuttled New York fellows as promising referee choices, Curley did not protest. He said the July the Fourth bout was a western fight, between western men, though Johnson was more midwestern than western. Therefore, a western referee seemed in order.

For instance, someone who lived and worked west of Kansas City would be fine. If so, that would rule out George Barton, the accomplished sporting editor of the *Minneapolis News*.

Johnson, however, liked Barton. He had been one of the few newspaper-men to write that Johnson would beat Jeffries in Reno.[6]

What's more, Barton when younger had boxed professionally and had been the third man in the ring for numerous bouts over the years.

Thus it is not clear why Barton failed to come to Las Vegas and report on a world title bout. It's quite possible that his newspaper had decided the trip would not be worth the expense. On the other hand, Barton may have gotten lost traveling to New Mexico. In his autobiography, Barton makes a brief mention of the 1912 fight and remarks that it occurred in Las Vegas—Las Vegas, Nevada.[7]

Ad Wolgast, it was soon learned, had sent word to Jack Welch that he wanted Welch to referee his title fight with Joe Rivers, also on July 4, in Vernon, California. "If Wolgast wants me to referee," said Welch, "I will certainly go to Los Angeles." Just as readers had digested that snippet of news, the *San Francisco Chronicle* arrived with this information: Jack Jeffries, Jim's brother, would be willing to act as the referee for the Wolgast-Rivers showdown that same day.

The great Jim Jeffries, it must be known, said several times that he possessed no interest in going to New Mexico to officiate a fight that featured the man who had clearly ended Jeffries's career.

Amid the fuss and folly of who might referee the fight, heartbreak occurred. Lester Smith—who had followed his father, Ed Smith, into sports writing—died of tuberculosis at the St. Anthony Sanitarium in Las Vegas on June 4. Smith, who was twenty, had come to New Mexico from Phoenix in May to join his mother and three sisters, who were already there with their father.

During the summer of 1911, Lester had gone to Phoenix where he appeared to be improving under the nursing care of his mother, Sedan Smith. The previous spring, young Lester had contracted pneumonia while reporting on the Chicago White Sox. The pneumonia developed into tuberculosis. Lester had been serving as a special correspondent for the *Chicago Post*. Before going to the *Post*, he had served a stint at the *Chicago Evening American*, where his father was the well-known sporting editor.[8]

The high altitude in Las Vegas was said to be too much for him and plans were being made for Lester to relocate to Dodge City, Kansas. He never made it. Young Lester died in Las Vegas on June 3. He was eighteen years old.[9]

Services were held June 5 in the chapel of the J. G. Johnson and Sons Funeral Home in Las Vegas. Tommy Cannon, the fight's ring announcer and Jack Curley's jack-of-all-trades, accompanied Lester Smith's body to Chicago on Santa Fe train no. 2. Ed Smith's mother and sister would meet the coffin, which would be placed in a vault to await the return of the Smith family after the fight.

Some people surely wondered why Ed Smith didn't make that sorrowful trip to Chicago with his son's body. Smith definitely was in the running to be the referee of a world championship boxing match. He did not want to leave Las Vegas should he be named; the opportunity was too big to walk away from.

Presumably, Sedan Smith, Ed's wife, understood her husband's actions through all this. Ed Smith was a newspaperman tried and true. Deadlines coursed his veins. If chosen to be the referee, he would make the fight deadline no matter what.

The referee list was passed around and around, with names added and others scratched off. Charles O'Malley, self-appointed errand boy, presented a revised list to both Johnson and Flynn. Ed Smith survived the scratching process. So did Ed Cochran, Jack Welch, and Mark Levy. Levy's name remained on the list, and the *Chicago Daily Tribune* reported, "All of New Mexico is anxious to have Mr. Levy serve as chief referee."

On June 13, out of nowhere, the ex-champ Jim Jeffries checked in. "I am out of the fighting game," Jeffries told DeWitt C. Van Court of the *Los Angeles Times*. "I would sooner sit by the ringside and see this fight than be the third man in the ring." Jeffries pushed Jack Welch of San Francisco to handle the Johnson-Flynn bout. Meanwhile, Welch was busy promoting himself to officiate the Wolgast-Rivers fight the same day.

When Welch decided to stay in California, it became a lock that Ed Smith would be named referee in New Mexico. Curley and the New Mexico Athletic Club urged him stay in New Mexico and accept that function.

"Ed Smith Named as Referee for Big Fight," the *Albuquerque Evening Herald* banner headline read. Smith accepted the referee position upon being notified that he had been chosen. Two days before, when the choice reportedly had been narrowed to himself and Jack Welch, Smith had voluntarily withdrawn.

Lester Smith's death must have been on his father's mind. He was encouraged to reaccept and by June 16 it was official: Edward Wallace Smith would be the third man in the ring.

Jim Flynn shrugged at the news. "Anyone in the bunch suits me," the Puebloan told a *Chicago Tribune* reporter. "I honestly don't care. Ty Cobb or Lillian Russell will do."

Making a decision hadn't been easy, readers learned. For seventy hours the Smith-or-Welch argument went on behind closed doors and it looked impossible for Curley and Johnson to choose between them.

John Wray's column in the *St. Louis Post-Dispatch* sorted the puzzling resolution this way: Curley had managed George Hackenschmidt, and Smith had refereed both of Hackenschmidt's championship wrestling matches with Frank Gotch. Curley managed Flynn: thus, Ed Smith would referee Johnson-Flynn.

Was it a sympathy vote that gave Ed Smith the job? That may have had something to do with it. However, Smith was experienced in the ring. And yet he did not have an unblemished record.

In 1910, Smith refereed a brutal forty-five-round, bloody lightweight brawl between Battling Nelson and Ad Wolgast. In the twenty-second round, Both of Nelson's eyes were swollen shut. At the start of the fortieth round, Nelson was nearly so blind that he mistook the ring post for his opponent.

At that point, Smith finally stepped between the two men and halted the fight. To the many spectators, the fight should have been stopped much earlier.

As for Jack Welch, the almost-named referee of the Johnson-Flynn fight, Welch decided instead to officiate the Wolgast-Rivers lightweight championship in California, held the same day as the championship in Las Vegas.

That bout was not one of Welch's better days in the ring. In fact, he should have turned down the job, for he was roundly criticized afterward. Delivering simultaneous blows, the two fighters—participants in an early-in-the-day, zero-sum game—appeared to have knocked each other out in the thirteenth round. Welch, with his back to Rivers who lay sprawled on the canvas, counted to ten and then awarded the victory to Wolgast. Welch said that Wolgast had started to rise before reaching the count of ten. Rivers fans roared in disbelief, believing Rivers had been fouled.

To add to the confusion, the timekeeper insisted that Wolgast had started to get up when Welch reached the count of four. Welch's ruling became the official verdict, which was argued about for years.

The naming of Ed Smith as the Las Vegas fight's official referee caused a newsman to be amused. There are, he said, so many "officials" connected with this battle that it should be called the official fight for the heavyweight championship of the world. There is an official promoter, official treasurer, official press agent, official photographer, and official announcer. There is also the official program, official cigar vendor, official soda-pop merchant, official stamp keeper, and official stenographer. Was this an official prizefight?

A bigger question was soon to be asked: Was this jewelry official?

CHAPTER 18

The Necklace

THIRTEEN DAYS BEFORE the Las Vegas fight, Jack Johnson and his wife were indicted by a federal grand jury in Chicago for alleged smuggling. Smuggling? The very word surely caused much of America to pause in wonder.[1]

Smuggling seemed a crime that belonged to rum-running pirates or those who sent convicts steel files baked inside blueberry pies. Smuggling did not at all appear to be the provenance of the heavyweight king of the world, a man who was said to possess the wealth of Croesus. And yet the Johnsons' string of jewels quickly became the most talked about baubles since 1884 when the French writer Guy de Maupassant penned a celebrated short story about a desperately coveted choker, as did O. Henry later.

Jack Johnson loved few things more than giving women gifts. Early in June of 1911, he had traveled abroad with Etta. They motored about the continent with Johnson's Chicago hireling, Charles Brown, doing much of the driving. In London, before the threesome sailed back to the States in September, Johnson paid $6,800 for a necklace with fifty-five white diamonds. Arriving at the port of New York, Johnson surely was asked by a customs agent if he had anything to declare.

Johnson responded with a smile and a back-and-forth shake of his head. Did he perhaps forget he possessed an expensive necklace? Not likely. In fact, he bragged to Etta how he had gotten past the customs inspector.

In spite of an inclination to spend big, Johnson had a frugal side, culti-vated by a boyhood in Galveston where his parents worked to make every penny count. He had gone through a lot of money since he fought Jeffries in 1910, and he didn't make that up in England as he had planned.

When he and Etta reached Chicago, Johnson stuck the necklace in a drawer of the couple's bedroom. Etta Johnson apparently was wearing another expensive necklace when she and Johnson stepped off the train in Las Vegas in late May. On that occasion, a reporter for the *Las Vegas Optic* wrote this: "The diamonds on her glittered like a row of electric lights."

Several attempts were made by Johnson to settle the case with payment of part of the duty and a penalty. The necklace was valued at $3,000 according to Johnson, and with the duty and the fine, the federal government declared it was due $6,000.[2]

An indictment followed. Authorities in Chicago said the indictment would not interfere with the July Fourth fight. Johnson was allowed to come forth with a $5,000 bond in Las Vegas, and after Independence Day he would be required to return to Chicago and plead to the indictment.

The biggest sigh of relief almost certainly came from Jack Curley. Trumped-up attendance promises had already put the fight on shaky ground. It wasn't as if Curley could line up just any boxer to face Flynn at this late date. Johnson was the drawing card. He alone was the reason the fight would be held.

On June 17, when Johnson was asked about the necklace, he told reporters in Las Vegas, "Possibly there will be a fine of $1,000 or something of the sort, although I have agreed to pay the full amount."

Two days later, Etta Johnson left Las Vegas in a hurry and traveled to Chicago. Rumor had it that she would face the grand jury herself to straighten out the mess.[3]

That did not happen and she returned to New Mexico.

The smuggling case simply would not go away. Johnson's fame and prominence, his wife's wiles, and an upcoming world championship prizefight were not going to stand in the way of the law.

Almost two weeks after the fight, when he returned to Chicago, Johnson was arrested by United States Marshal Edward Northrup. Johnson was charged with striking and intimidating a government witness in the criminal proceeding for smuggling, which was pending against him and Etta. If found guilty, Johnson faced a maximum penalty of $1,000 and one year in a federal prison.

Such an event added one more reason, to a growing number of reasons, why the US government was building a case to keep Johnson away from prizefighting anywhere in the United States.

Apparently, Johnson was given the chance to square matters with the government by handing over $9,000, a "mere bagatelle for Jack," said newspaper writer Robert Edgren. Johnson stalled, according to Edgren, "which is his nature, and the federal grand jury did the rest. Sometimes it doesn't pay to stall."

How did the government find out about the smuggled stones? Did someone snitch on Johnson? "I've been trying for a long time to find out who it was 'turned me up' in this matter," Johnson said. "Now I'll get the line on the friend who was so good as to tell on me and I feel that it will be worth $1,000 to me to know who that particular friend is."

On July 12, Johnson found that friend: Charles Brown, the black chauffeur in Johnson's employ. Brown had gone inside the Johnsons' apartment with the feds eagerly following and led them directly to the drawer where the necklace was stashed.

As soon as Johnson was indicted, Brown quit giving rides to the champion. On July 13, Brown entered Johnson's recently opened Chicago café, and as he did, Johnson confronted him and asked what he had told the grand jury. When Brown refused to answer, saying he had taken an oath to not talk about the case, Johnson punched him in the face. Brown was not about to mix it up with his boss. Brown stood just slightly more than five feet and was on the skinny side.[4]

Johnson was resting a foot on a spittoon on July 13, accepting congratulations for opening his café, when US Marshal Edward Northrup arrived and arrested Johnson on charges of striking a witness and talking about the case.

Johnson asked his chauffeur to leave the premises, but Brown did not go. One of Johnson's cronies showed Brown the door; Johnson departed as well—to his arraignment, where bond was set at $3,000.

Johnson's troubles following the Las Vegas fight continued. On July 22, he was charged with hitting Carson Hill, a black waiter employed at his café. According to Johnson, Hill had "short-changed" a patron.

The champion's trouble with chauffeurs didn't go away. On July 25, Johnson reportedly caught his replacement driver, Herman Kochfield, attempting to steal an extra tire from his boss's automobile while it was parked in front of Johnson's café. An argument ensued and Kochfield reacted by swinging at Johnson. Not a good idea. A single crunching blow by Johnson sent Kochfield to the sidewalk.[5]

The two physical altercations with his employed servants, brief as they were, seemed clear evidence that Johnson did not get nearly enough fistic action in New Mexico. His cornermen would be in agreement.

CHAPTER 19

Cornermen

EACH FIGHTER HAD assembled his retinue of towel swingers and ammonia-bottle wielders, proclaimed a newsman on July the Fourth. From all over the country these handlers and seconds had come to New Mexico.

On May 30, Flynn's then-trainer, Tommy Ryan, had sent a telegram to Jack Curley, who was in California to build up the fight to anyone he happened to see there. Ryan's telegram asked Curley to keep an eye out for a good "rubber," or masseur, to help out in Flynn's corner.

Through the years there have been numerous wrestlers named Abdul the Turk. The Turk that Curley engaged had wrestled some, but much of his life had been spent in boxing rings where he rubbed down the backs, shoulders, and legs of weary or cramped-up prizefighters.

As the July fight approached, praise for the Turk and his abilities immediately filled newspapers. One scribe raved, "Abdul is registered as a regular six-cylinder, sixty-horse-power human vibrator, and when he starts giving Flynn a rub down he will instigate enough electricity to light this pretty little village for a month."

Waiting for the Turk to actually appear in Las Vegas became a story in itself, similar to the advent of Tommy Ryan's long-awaited manifestation. Daily updates told in print of the Turk's journey to New Mexico. "Terrible Turk is Coming" blared one headline. As if accompanied by the sound of trumpets, the Turk finally disembarked in Las Vegas on June 12.

With Tommy Ryan's sudden bolting from the Flynn camp, Abdul the Turk took over as Flynn's chief trainer. The Turk was well Americanized, visitors to the Flynn camp saw immediately. He did not resemble a Turk in dress or in voice. Was he really from Turkey? No one seemed to know. The Turk, writers remarked, stuck close to Flynn. "He watches every move the Puebloan makes," an amazed writer noted.

The Turk, it was discussed often, had probably operated in more training camps than anyone in the fight game.[1] He and Flynn were old friends from their stays in California. But this Jim Flynn, the Turk pointed out to newsmen in Las Vegas, was practically a new Jim Flynn.

"Jim is working harder than any other fighter I have been associated with," the Turk said. "Do you know he used to be an inveterate cigarette smoker? He was puffing those things while training for all his fights on the coast, even in his important battles with Sam Langford and Jack Johnson. They tell me he refused to leave them alone even when training for Al Kaufman in Kansas City. Jim also used to like his beer."

The smoking habit hadn't vanished completely, it seemed. A few photographs of Flynn during his training in Hot Springs, Arkansas, had Flynn regularly puffing away on a cigarette, according to a St. Louis Post-Dispatch reporter.[2]

Flynn apparently cut out smoking following his victory over Kaufman. When he had a good chance of getting on top, he stopped drinking beer too, he admitted.[3]

The Turk told everyone who stopped by Flynn's camp that his charge deserved to bring the heavyweight title back to the white race. He was in excellent condition and still had more than two weeks to go. "He is a bear for work and is behaving fine. If confidence counts for anything, the July Fourth battle is already here."

During his time in Las Vegas, the Turk never failed to come up with a succession of bizarre training methods. For one exercise, he had Flynn lie on his back. The Turk would then place atop Flynn a chair that the Turk would straddle. That done, Flynn would hook his legs in the rungs of the chair. From there Flynn would attempt to work himself from side to side in order to raise the chair up in the air.

Not every reporter was sold on the relationship between Flynn and the Turk. The Turk had always been a strong Johnson booster. Only in the last week before the fight did the Turk say much to his charge or express his feelings. Yet on June 25, the Turk was considered the most rabid Flynn supporter in the camp, it was reported.

To inspire this change, and perhaps to caution him, the Turk's pep talk that day was this: "Johnson has got to be every bit as good as he was in his battle with Jeffries two years ago."

The self-assured Turk promised: "If Johnson has gone back at all, and is unable to go at top speed over twelve or fifteen rounds, he will be carried out of the ring on the Fourth."[4]

Nicknamed "Professor," Watson S. Burns was the chief trainer in Johnson's camp. Burns had trained Johnson before and after his fight with Jeffries. He had also guided quality fighters Joe Gans and Joe Wolcott. With Tom Flanagan managing the camp and Professor Burns leading the workouts, an air of professionalism surrounded Johnson's tune-ups.

Watson Burns talked a good deal, though he was normally quiet and businesslike. He was not a professor nor was he an educator. In fact, his education was minimal. He was, however, a reader. He was forever reading books on history. His favorite books were about Abyssinia, Egypt, and Carthage, tomes replete with the deeds and glories of black men.

Most of all, Burns was a student of the science of boxing. "I cannot explain Johnson's greatness," Burns said after they finished training one day. "I doubt if Johnson can explain it. Unless you call it a gift—an inheritance, Johnson has a knack for fighting. He was noted for his great defense. During his entire career he never had a beating. That is why Johnson is so well-preserved today. His opponents always hit him where he should have been, but wasn't. He packed a mean punch, but he seldom pushed for a knockout. He made the uppercut world famous as a ring punch."

Burns was a maker of prizefight champions. He had not boxed much himself but was a titleholder in another sport—billiards. Indeed, he was ranked among the world's greatest billiards players. A native of Missouri, Burns came to California with his family when he was nine years old. The family settled in Pasadena and he started playing billiards at eleven. He later went on the road for twenty years as a billiards player and then as a boxing trainer.

Biddy Bishop, the sporting editor of the *Tacoma Daily News*, also would serve as a second for Flynn. Before he became a newspaperman, Bishop appeared in just four bouts as a featherweight. In 1895, he attempted to slug it out with Denver Ed Woods in Texas, until a sheriff came into the ring and broke up the function. The two fighters then hiked to a nearby forest where they finished tangling.

Based on that brief experience, Flynn, for bewildering reasons, wanted Bishop to be close at hand on July the Fourth.

It was no secret that Jack Curley liked wrestlers. Just before the fight in Las Vegas, Dr. Benjamin Franklin Roller, who possessed a degree from a recognized medical school, came on board to assist Flynn. Roller had been a very good heavyweight wrestler. He had toured Europe with Curley in 1911. In a match against a grappler from India named the Great Gama, Roller found himself being hurled to the mat, a move that left the good doctor with three broken ribs.

That injury aside, Roller was the man Curley employed to prepare George Hackenschmidt for his celebrated wrestling bout with Frank Gotch in July 1911. Curley now asked Roller to come to Las Vegas and check out Flynn and inspect the Fireman's fitness.

"Flynn is in perfect condition," Roller told the *St. Louis Post-Dispatch*.

Could a wrestler actually help a heavyweight prizefighter? In 1912 wrestlers frequently picked up each other in the ring and slammed one another to the canvas.

Were such moves useful to a boxer? Curley must have been the only man on Earth who believed so. Thus, Dr. Roller would find himself in Flynn's corner on Independence Day.

Tommy Burns, the former world champion and no relation to Watson Burns, let journalists know some weeks before the fight that he would be helping Flynn in the ring.

Tommy Burns said he would be there to get Johnson's goat. What could Burns say to Flynn that would achieve a victory? That was the question of the hour for sporting writers everywhere. Few believed that Burns would turn Flynn into a champion overnight. In the end, Burns was a no-show, as was Jim Corbett.

Burns had promised to be there to pass out tips to Flynn and, it was said, check on Flynn's weight.

CHAPTER 20

Weighing In

THE BODY WEIGHTS of Johnson and Flynn became, almost immediately, Topic Number 1 whenever reporters visited the fighters' training camps. Newspaper editors seemed to believe that readers were itching to know what numbers on a scale might reveal about each man. Someone's weight, whatever it might be, was significant.[1]

Even more than ten decades ago, Americans were trying to watch their weight—and their waistline. Display advertisements and articles about the value of keeping trim were already surfacing on the pages of newspapers and magazines. Compared to today's standards, most of those proportional messages now would appear preposterous.

The "tapeworm diet," for example, a product of the early 1900s, suggested that people eat the sanitized eggs of tapeworms in order to shed pounds and be thin. By the same token, many of the men of the press were convinced that the poundage issue would play a key role on July the Fourth. Such thinking, of course, proved to be claptrap.

On June 4, Flynn reportedly weighed 204 pounds. Johnson weighed 233 pounds when he arrived in Las Vegas. Within a week Flynn came in at 195 pounds. Flynn let the *Kansas City Star* know that he had lost 14 pounds since he set up camp at Montezuma Springs.

"I weighed around 212 pounds during my Hot Springs vacation," the challenger said. After Hot Springs, Curley showed off the Fireman in Wichita, Denver, Colorado Springs, and Pueblo. Not once in those places did Flynn break a legitimate sweat.

"I guess I never went any higher than 209 stripped," Flynn told the *Kansas City Star*." I don't believe I will drop any lighter. Tommy Ryan said I will get under 190 when he had complete control of my work. I guess what he said will be proven correct."

Only a couple of weeks later, Ryan announced to all that Flynn was a swollen oinker whose hefty physique clearly qualified him as a "blubbery heavyweight."

Soon after moving into his Gonzales Street house, Johnson was said to be doing six to twelve miles of roadwork over the mountain roads every morning. He started his boxing and gymnasium work on May 3 and he did not miss many six-to-ten rounds of sparring. He said he had taken off 9 ½ pounds.

Johnson did the expected roadwork but he clearly was more comfortable in his outdoor ring. Flynn had a six-week jump on Johnson, as far as training went. Nobody was particularly worried about Johnson, least of all Johnson.

Any excess poundage either fighter acquired could easily be blamed on the portions on their plates. Both Johnson and Flynn were trenchermen of the highest rank.

The Colorado press seldom wrote anything negative about Flynn during the span before the fight. After all, Flynn made his home in the Rocky Mountain State.

"His stature and reach are a great benefit to him against a rangy, clever man such as Johnson, on account of his peculiar way of infighting," the *Pueblo Chieftain* reported. "In fact, Flynn is a larger man from every viewpoint than the once famous John L. Sullivan was when he was king of the hill. No one ever accused Sullivan of being too small for anybody."

"Flynn," the *Chieftain* reporter went on, "is working earnestly. He is not even reading what writers say, pro or con. Instead he is leading the simple life, and filling himself with the confidence that a white man will once more wear the heavyweight championship pugilistic crown."

Weight references took up newspaper columns everywhere. "Jack Johnson never has looked like a broiled lobster and never will," the *Chicago Evening American* printed on June 4. "He doesn't sweat when he works out. And so far as is noticeable he doesn't shed any of his superfluous avoirdupois."[2]

The issue of weight and size and endurance came to a head when both fighters were examined on June 16 by Dr. Edwin B. Shaw, former president of the New Mexico Medical Society.

"I regard Jim Flynn as one of the most magnificent specimens I have ever examined," Shaw effused. "His eyesight is normal, his heart and lungs normal in every particular. Likewise, his abdominal organs are normal. In fact, I do not find a single flaw in the man. He seems to have wonderful endurance. The altitude is not affecting him in the least and he certainly ought to be able to withstand a great deal of punishment."

To this, a *Kansas City Star* writer cracked, "It is a magnificent thing to be absolutely normal."

Shaw had practiced medicine for thirty years and was a member of the Santa Fe Railroad staff of surgeons. The doctor announced more or less the same thing about Johnson—with one striking exception: "His chest expansion is not up to the standard, which would lead one to fear a lack of endurance."

Shaw insisted Johnson was in good condition, but he worried about Johnson's so-called underdeveloped chest and Johnson's "poor wind." In fact, Shaw doubted Johnson would be able to go the distance on July the Fourth should the bout extend that far. This came from the *Kansas City Star* on June 19.

Information about the physical size and health of the two fighters surely drew a few laughs from readers on June 17 when a howler appeared in the *St. Louis Post-Dispatch*. An article about Dr. Shaw's findings said the good doc "eulogized" Flynn. Oh, well, R. I. P. Jim.

This much was known from the examinations: if Flynn remained his present weight, he would enter the ring many pounds above what he was reported to have weighed for any previous bouts, in which he was in good shape.

Flynn never had weighed more than 185 pounds for any match. His best weight recently was considered to be 175. Johnson's weight surpassed what he weighed at the Jeffries bout in 1910 or at any of his bouts. He was reported at the time as weighing 200 pounds.

Thoughts and comments about weight did not cease. "Johnson is no longer panther-like, as he was against Jeffries," a Denver reporter wrote. "His torso, instead of presenting the muscular leanness of someone physically fit, now resembles a barrel. Not that he has any lumps of fatty tissue showing. He is just big all over save for flank and calf, which never have been powerful looking. Now they look frail."

If Johnson was fat, Flynn was fatter. The *Los Angeles Daily Times* sent Flynn a picture of himself sitting on a fence. The caption said Flynn looked like a "fat old washerwoman." He weighed 195 pounds—and looked it. "His weight makes him slow and he will be short of wind should the battle go any distance," the Los Angeles reporter wrote. "All his work, which is honest, does not reduce his weight. He is too heavy for his inches."

Dr. Shaw told the *Kansas City Star* on June 18 that Jim Flynn was not fat. "I examined him last Saturday and in addition to finding him physically fit and sound, I doubt if he is carrying around more than 4 pounds of superfluous flesh. He was stripped when I weighed him and tipped the scales at 196. I consider him in excellent condition and do not see how he can take off more than a couple of pounds unless Manager Curley asks me to saw off an arm or leg."

Johnson said he would weigh 205 pounds when he entered the Las Vegas ring. That number sounded reasonable to all. Even so, Robert Edgren in a June 15 column for the *Evening World* asked this question: "Why is Johnson so fat?"[3]

Edgren answered his own query: "There are many reasons. He may be fat because he thinks he'll have an easy time beating up the little heavyweight. He may be fat because he doesn't think Flynn can last long."

Edgren continued: "He may be fat because he can't take the weight off. (Even after he went on a twelve-mile run, as he said he did so every day.)"

"Flynn may be fat," Edgren went on, "because the fight was already framed up (fixed), and it will go on according to plans. In that case, Johnson's condition wouldn't be important. So why should he do all that hard training?"

Johnson's chest at rest measured 40 1/2 inches. Flynn's chest revealed an even 39 inches. Johnson's chest expanded was 42 1/2 inches. Flynn's expanded chest was 41 ½ inches.[4]

The need for chest expansion was negated by the *St. Louis Post-Dispatch* on June 25. "If the high altitude has affected the champion's lung power, he is wonderfully adroit at concealing it."[5]

CHAPTER 21

Old Acquaintances

EVERY FEW WEEKS up to the time of the Las Vegas fight, newspaper writers nationwide began to dust off articles about the first bout between Johnson and Flynn, in 1907.[1] It was as if sports reporters felt that that five-year-old piece of the past might somehow offer a necessary means of comparison.

When the announcement came in early 1912 that Jack Johnson, the titular world heavyweight champion, would fight Fireman Jim Flynn, a battle-scarred knockabout, close followers of boxing matters must have been puzzled.

Why them again? Didn't those two guys already meet up with one another? Yes, they did once box each other, and the outcome was completely one-sided. So why were they squaring off again?

Only Jack Curley could answer that.

The pair first faced each other on November 2, 1907, in Coffroth's Arena, a well-known fight venue that sat near the north end of the San Francisco peninsula. It was named for a savvy, red-haired promoter, James "Sunny Jim" Coffroth.[2]

At that inaugural meet-up, Johnson weighed 192 pounds while Flynn came in at 174.

A genuine journeyman, Flynn was willing to take on almost anyone during the first decade of the twentieth century. Johnson was far pickier. Ambitious, he chose opponents with a purpose. His true target in 1907 was Tommy Burns, who then ruled the heavyweight division.

Johnson figured his fight with Flynn might very well lead to a shot at Burns's seat of domination. Flynn had mixed it up with Burns the year before in Los Angeles. That encounter was nothing short of savage. Burns sent the

Fireman reeling to the floor on three occasions. Each time, Flynn told his corner to "throw in the sponge," meaning he wanted the fight stopped and he wanted to quit.[3]

Nine minutes into the fifteenth round, Burns dropped Flynn to the canvas a fourth time. Pounded badly, Flynn was carted from the ring in a semiconscious state.[4]

Flynn had an equally unpleasant time with Jack Johnson in 1907. Their match was supposed to go forty-five rounds. The esteemed boxing writer Bill Naughton wrote, "No one dreams it will last that long."

Coffroth's Arena fans jeered Johnson because five months earlier the *San Francisco Chronicle* had published a story that said Johnson was going get married to a young woman from Sydney, Australia, with the rather unusual name of Lola Toy.[5]

"Jack Johnson to Wed White Girl" read a *Chronicle* headline on May 10, 1907.

Johnson paid no attention to the catcalls from spectators. For most of the fight he frolicked with Flynn, "like a terrier would with a rat," observed the Associated Press.

Always a brawler, Flynn had decided to rush in at every chance and trade punches with Johnson at close quarters, which of course was a bad idea. In the first round, Johnson, who fought with great guile, nearly closed Flynn's left eye. From that point on, the champion went after that eye with left jabs. Even with an eye partially shut, Flynn continued to make a beeline at Johnson. Johnson responded by landing blows to Flynn's head and jaw. He finally succeeded in closing Flynn's eye altogether.[6]

The fight swiftly turned into an exchange of ugly words, most of that coming from Flynn in the form of racial jeers. After realizing Johnson had the fight in hand, Flynn peppered the air with indignities. "You're a clever nigger, I wish I knew as much as you," Flynn sneered. Johnson laughed and said, "That's what I am. You are sort of a nasty white boy, ain't you?"[7]

The exchange of such back talk soon ended. Flynn, with but one eye, lowered his head and came at Johnson again, but nothing seemed to work. In the eighth round, the crowd heckled Johnson repeatedly for fully a minute. Johnson paid little mind.

Flynn found himself in a clinch during the tenth and, as a last resort, head-butted Johnson viciously. That brought a warning from Billy Roche, the fight's referee. At the finish of the penultimate round, Flynn clomped slowly toward his corner. He glanced at Johnson and growled, "You're an awful tough nigger."

When the eleventh round began, Johnson yelled derisively, "C'mon, Flynn. They [fans] are telling you to."

Flynn needed no urging from those attending. However, his left eye was secured tighter than the top of a pickle jar from repeated visitations of Johnson's gloves. A straight right to Flynn's jaw seemed to cut out any talking by the Fireman. But Johnson wasn't done with his opponent. This unmistakably had turned into an abattoir.

"Then came the eleventh round and the swift uppercut which meant taps for Flynn," Bill Naughton wrote in the *San Francisco Examiner*. "The last thing to hit the floor was the top of Flynn's head." Johnson had, as he famously put it, "knocked his opponent into tomorrow." It took officials four minutes to resuscitate Flynn. Two of Flynn's cornermen were needed to lug their fighter's banged-up body out of the ring.[8]

Johnson could have decked Flynn whenever he pleased in that fight. "He could do the same thing today," Naughton wrote of that night.

Referee Billy Roche told the press, "Johnson was the best man and outclassed Flynn in every department." Roche added, "The result would have been the same whether Flynn's eye was closed or not. Johnson is easily the best man in his class."

Afterward, Johnson said, "I knew I had him when I shut his eye. He is a game little boy, but too small for this class (heavyweight). Tommy Burns is my next man and I stand ready to fight him at any time."

Johnson left Coffroth's Arena that evening without a single mark on him.[9] Five years later, Flynn turned out a blatantly inaccurate and excuse-ridden newspaper story about his 1907 match with Johnson.[10] Assisted ably by H. W. Lanigan, Flynn said that he was a "green" fighter that night in California. (Truth: he had experienced fifty professional bouts before that one.)

Most astonishing, Flynn blamed the 1907 defeat not on Johnson's ring skills or his punching power but on, of all things, elevation. In other words, he should have trained in California and not in Colorado.

"When I began to prepare for my second battle with Johnson, I made up my mind I would not make the same mistakes again. I came to Las Vegas in plenty of time to get thoroughly used to the atmospheric conditions there."

Flynn, via Lanigan's typewriter, rattled on lamely to the press in 1912 about altitudinal inaccuracies in 1907. "I am not prepared to say how much the climatic conditions may have affected me or Johnson in our first battle. But I do know that Johnson, having been brought up in a low altitude, should have gained an advantage."

"If there is any advantage in climatic conditions—and I think most every well-posted fan will admit there is—then such an advantage exists."

Were those words simply hot air? The reporters on hand simply shrugged. None of them were "atmospheric authorities."

CHAPTER 22

Clickety-Clickety-Click

MORE THAN THREE hundred reporters descended upon Reno, Nevada, in the week before the long-awaited Johnson-Jeffries engagement.[1] Among several sitting beneath a sweltering Nevada sun were correspondents from England, Australia, and France.

They and others were there to watch Johnson topple Jim Jeffries for the much-awaited world heavyweight championship on July 4, 1910.

Between twenty-five and thirty journalists, plus four or five photographers, showed up in Las Vegas, New Mexico, for the Johnson-Flynn confrontation.[2] Why so few? Wary of the governor's stance, several sporting writers, as they were called a century ago, were not completely convinced the fight was going to happen.

Moreover, several newspaper publishers did not want to send a member of the press to far-off New Mexico unless they could be certain the governor would change his decree and let the fight go on. Which eventually did happen, of course.

To the more experienced reporters, the Las Vegas event seemed a sappy pairing from the moment it was announced. The bout did not appear at all significant as a premiere heavyweight championship should. In fact, some skeptical chroniclers early on believed a Johnson-Flynn card might not be on the up-and-up. At the time, the terms for a rigged prizefight were "frost" and "frame-up."

Some veteran boxing writers did appear in New Mexico on July the Fourth to tap out clickety-clickety-click at ringside. From there, the correspondents sent their work via telegraph to a deskman at their publications.

Among the better-known scribes present were Bill Naughton of the *San*

Francisco Examiner, Sandy Griswold of the *Omaha World-Herald*, John I. Day of the *Inter Ocean* (sometimes misspelled the *Inter-Ocean*), Harry Sharpe of the *St. Louis Post-Dispatch*, Walter Eckersall of the *Chicago Daily Tribune*, Otto Floto of the *Denver Post*, and Claude Johnston of the *Kansas City Star*.[3] Ed Smith of the *Chicago Evening American* would be there too, for certain, serving as referee for the match.

Frank A. "Fay" Young was the rookie in the group. A twenty-seven-year-old freelancer for the *Chicago Defender*, Young was one of the few black journalists on the scene.[4] Until he embarked on what would be a distinguished career in journalism, Young had worked as a Pullman porter and dining-car waiter.

In early May it was let known that the celebrated publisher William Randolph Hearst would be ringside. There were dozens of Hearst newspapers across the country, but just a few sent their sporting staffers to Las Vegas.

There is no evidence that Hearst actually made the trip to New Mexico. If true, his absence wasn't exceptional. Several boxing newshounds were no-shows. The Associated Press sent one man. Likewise did the Bain News Service, the first photo news service in the United States. David Anselberg, who photographed Flynn in Hot Springs, Arkansas, journeyed to Las Vegas for the fight.

Also appearing was Percival Francis Dana, a banty, Yoda-like gent often called the "Rembrandt of photography" or the "dean of boxing photographers."

Percy Dana traveled mostly about the West, where he captured on film prizefighters and their matches. In April 1912, the *Oakland Tribune* reported that Dana was issued a restraining order to stop taking photographs of baseball games. It seems another photographer had been awarded that privilege. In Las Vegas, Dana captured several images of Flynn and Johnson clinging to each other as they shuffled about the ring in what looked a lot like a slow waltz.

The fight generated little interest to the *New York Times*.[5] The *Times* did send a reporter but no byline identified him. All in all, disdain filled that newspaper's pages. "Johnson-Flynn Bout Regarded as a Joke" read one prominent *Times* headline the week before the contest.

In fact, the *Times* during that period frequently took an amused attitude toward prizefighting.[6]

Rather than give attention to the news of New Mexico, the newspaper detailed the 1912 boxing doings in New York City. In particular the *Times* made sure to provide news space whenever a lightweight named Leach Cross was involved.[7]

Cross had one of the best-known nicknames in the annals of boxing: the Fighting Dentist. Born Louis C. Wallach, on the Lower East Side of Manhattan, Cross graduated from New York University Dental School in 1907. He continued to box while maintaining a busy dental practice in the city. If he ever felt upset about the damage done to the teeth of an opponent, he never said so publicly.

On June 4, 1912, the Fighting Dentist faced George "Knockout" Brown at Madison Square Garden. Though Brown had KO'd many others, and held that much-vaunted record dear, he had never been dropped to the deck himself. That mark fell by the wayside this June night.

Twice Cross's left hand, which arrived point blank on Brown's mandible, sent the KO artist to the floor. On this occasion, Knockout wasn't knocked out, only knocked down. It is not known if the Fighting Dentist dislodged any incisors.

Otto Floto took charge of the sporting pages of the *Denver Post*, starting in 1898 and continuing until his death in 1929. Floto had little formal education and drank like a funnel. Loud and ornery at times, he never turned down a meal, particularly if someone else was paying.

Floto disdained punctuation and was nowhere near the stylist that the erudite Bill Naughton was. Floto had been hired by the *Post* supposedly because the owners liked his curious name.

John I. Day had bounced around the country, taking newspaper jobs here and there when he could, while trying to support his family. He wound up reporting in Chicago for the *Inter Ocean*.

Day's family included three sons and two daughters. His sons went into newspapering and his oldest daughter, Dorothy, announced that she might too. Her father, who could be a tyrant, told her no, a woman couldn't do that. But Dorothy Day went right ahead anyway. She founded the *Catholic Worker* newspaper and became world famous as a social activist. John Day's legacy was his daughter's remarkable life.

One of the best-known boxing writers in the early twentieth century did not travel to Las Vegas. William Barclay "Bat" Masterson, formerly a western sheriff and supposedly a skilled gunfighter, had settled in New York as the sporting editor of the *Morning Telegraph*. Masterson, who had an elevated opinion of himself, titled his column at the paper Hot Off the Bat. He wrote a good deal about the Johnson-Flynn bout without bothering to leave his office in Manhattan. Beginning with the fight's birth announcement, Masterson had nothing but scorn for the matchup.[8]

Boxing writers in 1912 had a vocabulary all their own. When a fighter spent time in a gym skipping rope, throwing a medicine ball, or punching a heavy canvas sack, he was doing "stunts."

A prizefight to most reporters was a "battle," or a "big battle," or frequently a "battleground." Now and then a fight was a "scrap" or a "go" or a "mill." Boxing was "milling" and the bell used to sound rounds was always the "gong." A fight that appeared to be fake was often called a "frost."

Correspondents who covered Johnson in 1912 had at their disposal a range of different epithets to describe him. By far the most popular was the "dusky." Close behind was the "dinge" and the "cinder." Johnson was also the "tar baby," the "chocolate champ," the "darkie," the "ink spot," the "big inky," the "big buck," the "big smoke," the "gorilla," the "Ethiopian," the "Congoman," the "Zulu cinder," the "African giant," the "coal," the "big coal," the "load of coal," the "caveman," and perhaps strangest of all, the "anthracite fistic wonder."

As reporters reached for one of these nicknames, the use of an apostrophe seemed to stump numerous of them. The spelling of "Li'l Artha," Johnson's nickname, appeared a half-dozen different ways in 1912—from "L'il Artha" to "L'l Artha" to simply "Lil Artha."[9] The root of that nickname was said to be Johnson's pet appellation for himself. However, several news reporters noticeably used it as a means of derision.

Though Jim Flynn had not worked for the railroad in several years, he was forever the "Fireman." On occasion he was the "Pueblo Coal Passer." One newsman called him the "Italian," which he was, and a few uninformed writers called him the "Irishman," though any Irish blood in Flynn's veins was questionable.

If Otto Floto was a character, W. W. "Bill" Naughton was the "dean" of boxing writers during the first two decades of the 1900s. Naughton was that, and more. He wrote two books on milling. A natty dresser, Naughton spoke with a purring accent, the result of growing up in New Zealand.[10] One of fourteen children, as a youth he stood out as a boxer, oarsman, runner, swimmer, and marksman.

There existed an imperious quality to Naughton's prose, perhaps because others considered him king of pugilism's writers. In fact, when Naughton arrived by train in Las Vegas, a respectable crowd came to the station to meet him.

In a way it is surprising that Naughton observed the Las Vegas match instead of attending the Ad Wolgast and Joe Rivers bout on the same day at the same time. Naughton explained that his being in Las Vegas was because dozens of sporting writers had asked him to get a quick look at Johnson; if he appeared as a champion, they would make the trip to New Mexico.

Grantland Rice, America's most celebrated sportswriter during the 1920s and '30s, was a rookie columnist for the *Atlanta Journal* in 1912. As might be expected of a newspaper set deep in the Jim Crow South, the *Journal* refused to pay attention to the scuffle and sent no one to New Mexico.

CHAPTER 23

Disturbing Days

WITH THE ADVENT of the prizefight fast approaching, several Las Vegas businessmen, the city's mayor, and the chief of police hurriedly worked overtime to make the town not only law-abiding indoors but spanking clean out of doors.[1]

The police force spent many hours keeping order and rounding up card sharks, grifters, and a growing clutch of light-fingered thieves.

Restrictions of all kinds were upheld. Gambling houses were shut down until the fight ended and spectators departed. Information about the usage of brothels was not made public.

Mayor Robert Taupert announced that he would revoke the license of any hotel or rooming house that attempted to charge exorbitant rates. Cots were available at many homes for those who couldn't afford tickets. Folding cots sold for $1.50 at the Ilfeld General Store. Many of the cots filled hallways of homes. Vagrants, drunks, and hobos were either jailed or encouraged to leave the city. No one was spared. Ed Ryan, a bindle stiff, was told to hit the road, the Las Vegas Optic reported in its City News column.

Taupert instructed policemen to stop citizens from throwing rubbish in alleys and in vacant lots. Defiling those areas would lead to arrest, the mayor said. All cans and trash had to be kept in a barrel or some type of receptacle before being hauled away. Stables needed to be tended, for the smell some days was stronger than Hercules. Flies showed up everywhere in the West that summer, it seemed. Platoons of these tiny nuisances filled the air like Napoleonic soldiers in a formation drill.

To take care of various issues, Taupert appointed Jack Curley to serve as assistant chief of police. Because Curley had been around large throngs

before, the mayor believed the promoter would be able to recognize potential
mischief-makers. Amused, Curley's friends presented him with a gold badge,
which he wore often.

Weeds that popped up within the city limits would not be tolerated. Police
Chief Ben Coles was determined that every dandelion, finger grass, and
unappealing plant in Las Vegas be yanked up before the main event began.
Coles began notifying property owners and real estate agents that all rank
vegetation must be extracted or prosecution in the police court would follow
without delay.[2]

Mayor Taupert, who apparently knew something about botany, decreed
that every flowering weed needed to be removed from the ground before it
had a chance to seed. Weeds were said to be a health menace, and were
believed to be a breeding ground for germs of all kinds.

It is difficult to understand how pristine alleys and uprooted chickweed
patches would make a difference in a world championship prizefight. Most
fans likely did not give a whit about the contents of scruffy plots of land or
hobos showing up now and then. Such matters would certainly not affect the
Johnson-Flynn goings-on.

Of much greater concern in Las Vegas during the days before the fight
were a number of disturbing incidents. Frank Herrera, a liquor dealer in Las
Vegas, found himself in a gun duel on a city street with another liquor dealer,
Charles Alellon. Herrera was shot in the hip and was in serious condition at
a Trinidad hospital.[3]

A few days later, Mrs. Alcaria Montoya, a mother to several children,
became deranged one morning and poured cooking oil on her clothes. With
the strike of one match she set herself on fire. As she ran along the streets on
the west side of Las Vegas, Mrs. Montoya's screams attracted Henry Mont-
simer, who swiftly wrapped the demented woman in a blanket and extin-
guished the flames. She was carried to a nearby home. It was thought she
would die. There was no evidence of an accident or an explosion in her home.
It was thought she attempted self-destruction while temporarily insane.[4]

Suffering under the delusion that someone had taken his money and
might take his life, George Demitriz, a passenger on the Santa Fe no. 2 train,
experienced a fit of insanity as his train car crossed Glorieta Pass. Santa Fe
officers notified the Las Vegas station. When the train arrived in Las Vegas,
two officers were there to meet it and take Demitriz into custody.

Before that took place, Demitriz pulled a penknife from his pocket and attempted to jab an artery in his neck. Officers quickly handcuffed Demitriz and brought him to Las Vegas Hospital.[5]

It took the strength of four men to hold him down in bed.

Two days before the prizefight, sheepherders in an area just south of Las Vegas came upon the body of a grown man. The remains were badly decomposed and apparently had been lying there for more than a month. The corpse appeared to have been clubbed about the head with a rock or a heavy club and bashed to death.

The man's teeth were extracted by deputy Secoundio Romero in hopes that the teeth might be of use in identifying the body. The man evidently was a stranger in Las Vegas, as his clothes did not bear the trademarks of local merchants. This was the first murder committed in San Miguel County in more than two years.

The immolation of Alcaria Montoya, the self-stabbing of George Demitriz, and the discovery of a mutilated corpse in all likelihood did not sit well with Jack Curley. The promoter surely feared such events would scare potential spectators from attending the fight.

Not all news stories in Las Vegas were so ghastly. Small criminal cases were occupying the attention of the district court and most sessions proved uneventful. In early May, Las Vegas police arrested Rufino Garcia for assault with a deadly weapon used upon Nieves Maes, who, it was believed, had died.

A coroner's jury was called to determine exactly how Maes had met his death. Just as the jury was about to render a verdict that would accuse Garcia of murder with a firearm, Maes regained consciousness and walked into the courtroom. His face bore a puzzled expression.

Though shot in the arm, Maes apparently had been unconscious all along.

Such a surprising scene freed Garcia of a serious criminal charge. At the sight of Maes, gales of laughter swept the courtroom. Judge David J. Leahy, who was on the bench that morning, could not resist the desire to smile.

CHAPTER 24

Getting Closer

IN THE EARLY afternoon of July 2, at Ed Smith's request, Johnson and Flynn met up with the referee at La Castaneda Hotel. The purpose of this get-together was to discuss all questions that might arise when the two men entered the ring. It was agreed early on that both men should use their own gloves. There would be no wrestling, no hugging, and of greatest significance, no clinching in the ring.[1]

Johnson insisted and it was agreed that should there be any interference, such as a policeman, a rainstorm, or a riot, Smith would render a decision in favor of the man having the best of the contest. Both fighters agreed that there be no holding and hitting at any time and that they must agree to break at the command of the referee.

Showing no jitters, Johnson on the eve of the fight motored in his car to the arena. There he watched a match between lightweights Rudy Unholz and Stanley Yoakum. Johnson sat at ringside in silence. His face wore a look of tedium as the two young fighters pulled and hauled through twenty rounds that ended in a draw.

Curley had originally signed a contract for one-day use of the arena. Which does not mean one day prior. It is not clear how Curley got around that agreement. With so many things on his mind, it's entirely possible Curley forgot about the contract and used the arena a day early.

As Johnson had done, Flynn that evening climbed into his auto and drove off alone, not to the arena but to La Castaneda Hotel. He arrived there clad in a brilliant red sweater, according to Flynn disciple Charles Patrick of the *Pueblo Star-Journal*.

The ever-worshipful Patrick wrote, "The sweater showed to advantage the lines of Jim's huge chest and powerful shoulders." Patrick clearly could not control his adoration: "As Flynn marched about the hotel porch, his springy steps and sun-burned face indicated perfect health. Flynn was followed by a mob of well-wishers."

Flynn and Ed Smith talked briefly at the hotel about the gloves to be used. Those gloves would be five ounces, with soft bandages allowed. Flynn's stop at La Castaneda was a short one. Before dark he was back at Montezuma Springs, where visitors were discouraged.

On the morning of the fight, readers learned, both men ate broiled chicken for breakfast. Flynn spent the forenoon in his cottage. Meanwhile, C. W. Patrick, Flynn's biggest backer, spent a few hours inspecting the arena.

The ring ropes and the net posts were wrapped in red, white, and blue cloth. All seats were at ground level. By today's standards, not exactly sought-after perches. The canvas sides of the arena were double walls, some ten feet high. That was apparently done to shut off the view of those not provided with credentials or tickets. The structure, wrote Patrick, strongly resembled a traveling big top, a description that ultimately turned out to be quite accurate. Patrick wrote that the fight would draw ten thousand people. On that, he was not at all accurate.

How relaxed were the two gladiators? At high noon on July the Fourth, Johnson and his camp's supervisor, Tom Flanagan, staged a foot race and coal-shovel duel on the right-of-way in downtown Las Vegas.[2] An estimated one thousand spectators stood by and watched in glee. To those who inquired, Johnson gave his weight as 214 pounds. Flynn would eventually enter the ring at 194 pounds.

The temperamental sides of the two men were distinctly different. Johnson was jolly, carefree, and apparently without a worry.[3] He was the cynosure of all eyes through the day, rubbing elbows with the home folk and passersby every time a train thundered up and hissed as it neared the Las Vegas station.

As the Fourth of July edged close, a carnival-like atmosphere took hold of the town. Souvenir stands displayed pennants and pictures of Flynn and Johnson. Food vendors hawked hamburgers, hot dogs, and soft drinks. All betting took place in an office on Center Street, managed by John O. Talbott, the betting commissioner. From almost the day the fight was announced in January, the odds of Johnson winning remained at 2/1. Few bettors saw much use in deciding otherwise.

Small betting and small people highlighted the presence of the holiday's morning.

CHAPTER 25

A Very Short Warm-Up Act

JACK CURLEY HAD spent a good amount of time seeking a high-level under-card for his July Fourth creation.[1] Curley wanted two talented and well-seasoned fighters who would entertain fans and bring excitement to his arena before Johnson and Flynn took center stage.

In May, Curley traveled to Los Angeles in an effort to land the Ad Wolgast–Mexican Joe Rivers world lightweight championship bout as his Las Vegas "curtain-raiser."

Curley would have to "pull a lot of strings—and curtains—for that to happen," according to the *Albuquerque Evening Herald*. The promoters of the California fight were surely amused at Curley's proposal to make the Wolgast-Rivers contest a divertissement to be set somewhere in the desolate stretches of the far-flung West.

Cajoling as best he could, but surprising no one, Curley failed to lasso the lightweight title showdown and have it moved to Las Vegas. Thus, the Wolgast-Rivers battle would remain in Vernon, California, close by Los Angeles, also on the afternoon of July the Fourth. H. W. Lanigan dismissed the rejection as poppycock. He boasted preposterously in print that Wolgast-Rivers would "be completely overshadowed by the bout in Las Vegas."

The California match turned into a wild affair watched by eleven thousand spectators. That figure would turn out to be almost four times the number of fans who would be present at the New Mexico arena.

Not only did that California crowd dwarf the Johnson and Flynn count, but the fight between Wolgast and Rivers would go down as one of the most exciting episodes in boxing history.

When the two fighters hit each other at the same time in the thirteenth round, Wolgast fell to the canvas atop Rivers. The referee, Jack Welch, stepped in and counted Rivers out and raised Wolgast's arm as the winner. Welch, it turned out, apparently did not have a clear view of the two-man pileup, and yet he decided to award the contest to Wolgast.

Rivers and his many supporters screamed that Wolgast was guilty of a foul. To prove his claim, in his dressing room after the fight, Rivers pulled down his boxing trunks and showed reporters the aluminum protector that covered his testicles. A distinct dent was revealed.

Unable to sign a pair of prizefighters of any note for a preliminary bout on July the Fourth, Curley eventually called upon two regional pugilists. This was not a big deal. In fact, it was quite small, for both of the contenders stood a good deal less than five feet tall.[2]

Of the many inane sideshows associated with the New Mexico fray, the yoking of a pair of children on the same bill as a global heavyweight championship ranks as one of the wackiest contrivances in all the chronicles of fistic performances.

Curley was aware that two brothers from Colorado Springs, Fred and Kenneth Day, were competent little boxers. They were certainly little. The Day boys, ten and twelve years of age respectively, weighed sixty-two and fifty-eight pounds. They had been trained in miniature fisticuffs by their father, Alec Day, whose weight was said to be well over two hundred.[3]

The senior Day was a pressman for Way Out West, a printing and stationery firm in Colorado Springs. It's likely he helped to promote his sons for Way Out West, which published both daily newspapers in Colorado Springs. In mid-June, Curley, desperate for an opening act, sent a letter to the boys' father explaining a plan to showcase his sons in the ring.

In an effort to seal the deal, Curley added this incentive: the brothers would be included in the motion-picture scenes in the arena "before and after the main battle." Impressed by Curley's offer, Alec Day wrote Curley that he and his sons would come to Las Vegas and he would serve as the referee for the lads. If for some reason he couldn't make the trip (presumably a remote possibility), the senior Day would send a responsible adult to accompany the youths and to look out for their welfare in New Mexico.

The Day brothers had something of a reputation in the West, where they had appeared in several pugilistic demonstrations. They were considered the most youthful exponents of glove work to be found anywhere, on authority from the Colorado Springs Gazette, which of course was overwhelmingly biased.

According to the youngsters' father, Kenneth Day and Fred Day (whose given name was Ferdinand) had won twelve gold medals and seven silver loving cups for their skills with padded mitts. They had been advertised as the "pin and the pennyweight champions of the world" and "the youngest boxers in America." One reporter described them as "midgets."

The Day clan arrived in Las Vegas on the third of July aboard the Stewart Special, a passenger train that consisted of four sleeping cars, a day coach, and a baggage car fitted out as a commissary. In Las Vegas, the Stewart Special sat parked, to be used as a hotel by special ticketholders.

Just prior to the introduction of the two tykes, a six-foot-six galoot climbed through the ropes and strutted to the center of the ring. Although Cass Tarver had not experienced a sanctioned bout in his life, he was said to be among the best fighters to come out of tiny Anson, Texas. Stuffed with self-praise, Tarver had journeyed uninvited to Las Vegas to challenge in person the winner of the Johnson-Flynn hoop-dee-doo.

Those seated in the Las Vegas arena did not quite know what to make of this outlier. Who on earth was he? More to the point, who permitted him to proclaim his intentions? No one seemed to know. Bewilderment and tepid applause greeted this extra large–size mystery man.

The moment Tarver left the premises, the Day brothers went at it. The siblings' punching display drew a combination of raucous laughter and appreciative cheers. The Days surely returned to Colorado with a lifetime of fond memories. Cass Tarver returned to Texas with no memories at all.

Against all odds, Tarver somehow gained his first recognized professional fight four months later. He went up against a far more experienced heavyweight. Carl Morris was one of the many White Hopes during the Johnson era. From Sapulpa, Oklahoma, Morris was known as the Sapulpa Giant. Tarver faced an onerous task.

On November 15, 1912, the two men fought a ten-rounder in Shreveport, Louisiana. During the second round, Tarver rocked Morris with a shot below the belt. That was followed by a second punch to the same spot. Morris fell to the floor with an agonized look. There was no need for officials to check his aluminum protector.

The referee helped the Oklahoman to his feet, disqualified Tarver, and gave Morris the victory. The record book shows that Cass Tarver's professional boxing career ended there.

CHAPTER 26

Antic Climax

WITH A NOTICEABLE slowness, small clusters of fans drifted into the Las Vegas fight grounds on Independence Day. Because there were 17,950 seats in the enclosure, no one hurried to claim a chair in such a vast and mostly vacant setting. The betting was hardly brisk. Johnson remained a clear 2/1 favorite.

On nearby streets, shillabers in great numbers continued to peddle souvenirs.[1] You could buy almost anything, from miniature boxing gloves to Navajo blankets. Straw hats known as "boaters" or "skimmers" decorated nearly every attending male. The same went for bow ties. Female spectators—fewer than one hundred, it was believed—wore long Edwardian summer dresses. On their heads were wide-brimmed floral hats, mainly to keep the sun off their faces. Thick cigar smoke had already begun to cloud the air, which remained feverishly warm.

A few minutes before 2:00 p.m., a chillingly loud and unexpected crunching sound filled the atmosphere. A giant telegraph pole that stood near one corner of the ring was interfering with the view of fans behind it. Curley, overly eager to take care of customers, especially those in the twenty-dollar seats, ordered for the pole to be removed. A handsaw was eventually produced.

Seconds later, the falling timber crashed down upon an empty seat. A spectator named Dave Finkelstein, a businessman from Colorado Springs, only seconds before could have been found in that chair. Miraculously, he leaped out of his seat just in time to avoid being killed.

Flynn was the first boxer to arrive at the arena. A Mexican band greeted him with "All Coons Look Alike to Me," music Flynn loved to hear. The composer of the ragtime-like tune was, surprisingly, a black man named Ernest Hogan, also known as Ernest Reuben Crowdus.

Hogan was a veteran of minstrel shows, a comedian and a dancer who claimed he put the music on paper, even though someone else wrote it. Hogan was in good company; Johnson and Flynn were not their full names either. Johnson was born Arthur Jack Johnson, in Galveston, Texas. Flynn came into this world in Hoboken, New Jersey, bearing the name Hector Chiariglione. At some point he took the name Andrew Haymes, until finally Jim Flynn stuck.

At 2:35 p.m., fight announcer Tommy Cannon climbed into the ring and pointed out a handful of notables in the arena. Among the first to be saluted seemed a natural for this Wild West afternoon. Judge Casimir Welch was a colorful cog in the Kansas City Democratic machine of the Pendergast era.

For more than thirty years, Welch controlled thirty-six precincts populated with African Americans. The judge was known for bullying and beating up political rivals. One of those rivals Welch shot and wounded in a street battle. Welch's sideline was promoting prizefights.

Suddenly Tommy Cannon boomed out, "Several hundred ladies have graced this occasion by their attendance. Please remember gentlemen and take care when using certain language or shouting distasteful things during the fight."

As was the norm for weeks prior to this match, exaggeration prevailed. Most likely there were far fewer than "several hundred ladies on hand." Fifty to one hundred women might be more accurate. This much was true: most of the women who took seats in the arena had come to see Jack Johnson.

When the two fighters entered the ring at 2:45 p.m., it was plainly apparent that the crowd favored Flynn. His appearance brought loud hurrahs, though nowhere near the thunderous demonstration Jim Jeffries had been given at Reno. Then, as now, Johnson received the plaudits of a few dozen fans. That same satisfied smile played about the champion's lips, while Flynn appeared to be in a good humor as he strutted about the arena, greeting friends. Spotting Etta Johnson, Flynn shouted, "Ain't you pulling for me, Mrs. Johnson?" The champion's wife smiled faintly but said nothing. Earlier, at Johnson's request, Etta had been moved to another seat in order to be nearer to his corner.

It was difficult to understand what Flynn had in mind when, from his corner, he called to Johnson, "Will you shake hands, Jack?"[2] In prizefighting, that act is de rigueur. Perhaps Flynn wanted to unnerve the champion. In response to Flynn's offer, Johnson issued a flat, apathetic "no." It was the kind of tone a diner in a restaurant would use to turn down a waiter's suggestion of cold soup. A staged photograph taken earlier does show the two men shaking hands.

A couple of seconds before the first round, a spectator fired a revolver into the air and a great cry went up: "That'll scare the skin off the black beggar," someone shouted.[3] The noise of the gunshot was similar to the sound of doom that had cracked the air in Reno in 1910.

Then, for some reason, no one could find the ring gong. Mild hysteria among the timekeepers followed. It was 2:47 p.m. when the missing gong was finally located.

A minute later it sounded.

CHAPTER 27

A Misbegotten Mess

WITHOUT FURTHER ADO, Jim Flynn, his head bent downward, raced full throttle across the ring to kick off round one. As if waiting for a train, Johnson kept watch in his corner, biding his time. His arms were draped casually across the ropes. Not one scintilla of fear marked his visage.

Standing at the ready in Flynn's corner was Chick Coleman, of all people. Had the chef from Flynn's training camp gone to the arena to thrust a sandwich at the Fireman, if so needed? Not likely. Coleman's appearance as a second remains one of those mysteries that leaves mankind with a sense of absolute bewilderment.

In the weeks preceding the bout, Flynn doubled down numerous times on his vow to not bring the battle to Johnson by using rushing tactics. So much for that pledge. This had all the earmarks of a reboot. Evidently, Flynn had forgotten the tutorial that Johnson delivered in 1907. The Fireman's rushing labors back then had caused him to wind up on his keister, blood spattered, and for all intents and purposes, dead to the world.

From the very early moments in Las Vegas, Flynn worked from a crouch, much like a man stooping about an attic in search of an heirloom. The Fireman's goal, now quite obvious, was to get under the champion's nose and do so swiftly. Always a superb defensive heavyweight, Johnson met Flynn's early charge by pushing the challenger away as if he were a buzz-happy mosquito.

While Flynn drew closer, Johnson flung a stiff left to the Fireman's face. Blood trickled down one cheek. Johnson smiled and continued to fight, but with care. Meanwhile, Flynn backed Johnson against the ropes. The champion rewarded him with a right that bequeathed a deep cut beneath Flynn's left eye. If Flynn possessed a playbook for this contest, he surely forgot to open it.

Round two brought the first signs of head-butting by Flynn. He camou-flaged that maneuver by clawing and cursing like a madman, ignoring warn-ings by referee Ed Smith.[1] Wearing a newsboy cap and a long-sleeve white shirt that did little to hide an expansive stomach, Smith clomped about the ring in a lagging manner, a cigar permanently parked in the right corner of his mouth.

Johnson sent sharp jabs that stung the Fireman at least five times. One of those punches caused the Puebloan's head to snap back.

A battle of blows and words took over. The two men talked to each other and to spectators in the seats. When Flynn finally took a stool in his corner, crimson fluids flowed from his mouth like a rolling creek.

In the third stanza, Flynn once again beelined straight for Johnson. The champion reacted by grasping the Fireman at the shoulders and holding him at bay, "all the while grinning like an ape," a *New York Herald* journalist wrote. Flynn spat red as Johnson let loose a volley of lefts and rights. Already this appeared to be unspectacular theater.

Johnson opened the fourth by belittling Flynn with comments. In response, Flynn twice hooked a right to Johnson's cheek. Those two blows seemed to nettle the champion. Unbothered, Johnson gave the crowd a wide smirk and then a wink. In the meantime, he peppered the air with bursts of sly remarks that seemed to annoy Flynn.

"Darlin," he called to his wife, "What we hav'n for supper tonight?"

Once again Flynn hurried in tight, but he was met with right and left uppercuts. "Here's more," the champion urged. With that, Johnson shook Flynn with a few whomps to the Fireman's midsection.

It was widely known in boxing that Flynn sucked on orange slices between rounds.[2] That wasn't going to happen this afternoon. Too much was at stake.

To further goad Flynn, Johnson stuck out his own belly and gestured to Flynn to blast away at it. Laughter in the arena flew like sparks. When the gong tolled the round's end, bright red streaks decorated much of Flynn's face and neck

Flashes of the 1907 fight with Johnson must have already entered Flynn's brain by the fourth. It was likely that his mind, however, did not process the words of philosopher George Santayana: "Those who do not remember the past are doomed to repeat it."

Nonetheless, Flynn moved in and delivered half a dozen punches to

Johnson's midsection. Johnson grinned and even winked. He made no attempt to protect himself. Instead, he gestured to Flynn to try again. To further bring joviality to those in the arena, Johnson let go of Flynn's hold and clapped his gloves together like a happy schoolgirl.

The atmosphere now was laden with hate. "I can't fight while the nigger's holding me," Flynn complained to Ed Smith. Johnson glanced at the men in his corner and indicated this altercation might go on all day.

During the sixth round, Flynn apparently decided that his head was his best weapon to gain a victory. Three times he came at Johnson, leaving his feet to strike the champion skull first. The Fireman justified employing this lift-off strategy by again grousing aloud that Johnson was clutching him. Smith responded by once again warning Flynn. Clearly, the challenger in desperation was trying to find a loophole to stem the beatdown he was receiving.

That whipping resulted in scorching lefts and rights, which caused Flynn to once more snarl that Johnson was hanging on to him. Visibly angry, Johnson unloaded a series of well-placed thumps to the challenger's torso. Such shots across the bow appeared to shake up Flynn.

When the Fireman repaired to his corner, a support group worked on his bashed-in physiognomy. Once more Flynn's cornermen sternly warned him to cease the head bonking.

On June 3, Ed Smith had written a column that Flynn was being coached to bump hard with his head as he went into clinches. Tommy Ryan was not yet in Las Vegas, so it was not known who advised Flynn to do this. Smith wrote: "Johnson is nearly a head taller than Flynn, and is likely to get many a welt and jolt under the chin, provided Jim can get under or through the champion's guard."

As if merely rapping on someone's door, Johnson in the seventh round landed a dozen rapid-fire lollops to Flynn's glum-looking countenance.[3] A spectator seated near the ring shouted for Johnson to end things.

"Y'all wait a minute," Johnson shouted.

As if turning his attention to the matters at hand, Johnson issued a steady drumbeat on the Fireman's mug. This time blood dripped profusely from Flynn's nose. In desperation, he flew anew at Johnson. Once again, head first.

"Stop the butting," Smith said as he shook his finger in Flynn's face. "Stop it or I will disqualify you." Hollow words, those. They had been submitted on two or three previous occasions in this now tiresome mismatch. Each time without recourse.

"Stop the nigger from holding me all the time," Flynn growled in return. "He's grabbing me like this." Flynn held out his blood-spattered arms as if to collar Johnson. Ed Smith motioned for the two men to get back to fighting again. When the gong rang out, Johnson had not a fleck of blood on him. In the eighth, Flynn immediately launched himself off the floor in one more futile attempt to lower the boom on Johnson's cranium. "Kangaroo hops," one sporting writer called the bounding display. Nowhere in any boxing instructional manual can such a technique be found. At that time, head-butting—like rabbit-punching, foot-stepping, corkscrew-jabbing, elbowing-to-the head, and other dishonorable techniques—had no place in respectable prizefights. To Flynn's repeated head knocks, Smith once more for good measure voiced what had become a weary refrain: "Stop or I will disqualify you."

To guard against the noggin-butting, Johnson kept Flynn at arm's length in the ninth round. Johnson surely realized now that the Fireman had no chance in this championship. Still, caution prevailed. Meanwhile, Flynn edged closer toward the bigger man and high-jumped virtually a foot off the floor. His battered bean struck in the vicinity of Johnson's mandible, causing little damage.[4]

Moments after the ninth began, Fred Fornoff, captain of the New Mexico Mounted Police, decided that this foul-filled mayhem had to cease. Fornoff apparently believed he had to do something, for Ed Smith appeared incapable of terminating the morass before him.

Turns out the biggest sporting event on the globe was no better than a basement smoker in the local Odd Fellows lodge hall.

With a ten-gallon hat perched on his head, Fornoff sprang from his ring-side seat and stumbled into the ring. Accompanied by a pack of his mounted troops, and by the Las Vegas chief of police, Fornoff brought the embarrassing altercation to an unpleasant and controversial finish.

By taking the law into his own hands, Fornoff let Smith—and anyone else who could hear the captain shouting—know that these shenanigans were no longer a boxing contest. Flynn's foul tactics made its continuance impossible.[5]

A bevy of lawmen now flooded the ring, along with the handlers of both fighters. The uniformed deputies were joined by an assortment of semi-officials, including town marshal Ben Coles. No one seemed to have any idea what was going on or what to do within this human maelstrom, this early-day mosh pit.

For several roiling minutes, Kafkaesque chaos reigned. Somehow, Ed Smith told Tommy Cannon to announce that this heavyweight championship, six months in the making, was over, and that Jack Johnson had won easily.

Down the rabbit hole Flynn went. The tectonic plates had not shifted.

Wearing gobsmacked expressions, spectators stood up sluggishly. Booing, hissing, and hooting pervaded the atmosphere. Now and then someone clapped. Here and there a faint cheer rose up.

All of Jim Flynn's training—his endless running along Las Vegas roads, his endless pounding of punching bags big and small, his sparring, rope-jumping, sit-ups, and medicine-ball hurling—was for naught. Flynn's many promises of triumph and his tiresome hubris vanished the moment the Fireman resorted to low-down, grossly unfair mauling.

Such was the only way Flynn knew he might have the narrowest chance of winning. No one anywhere accepted this plan. In fact, much of the country, when hearing of the outcome, were split between disgust and dismay. There would be no celebration afterward. No party, no nothing.

CHAPTER 28

Shouts, Shots, and Megaphones

ON JULY 4, 1910, in a contest for the world heavyweight title, defending champion Jack Johnson delivered an unmerciful pounding to Jim Jeffries, then the greatest of all White Hopes.

This happened in front of twenty thousand disbelieving spectators. In his heyday, Jeffries had broken opponents' ribs in the ring and had never suffered the indignity of being knocked down. In Reno, Johnson floored Jeffries twice and stood over him with a look of extreme satisfaction.

Following the unexpected thrashing of an American idol, violence erupted across the country.[1] "Rioting broke out like prickly heat all over the country," the *New York Tribune* reported. White people were sore and angry that the undefeated and much-admired Jeffries had lost that day while black people were jubilant that Johnson had won.

At least eleven and perhaps as many as twenty-six people would die before the bloody disorder ended. Hundreds more were hurt, almost all of them black.

The nationwide ruckus following the Johnson-Flynn goings-on was far calmer, though it was not without fatalities and assorted incidents of rage and fury.

In Kansas City, two black youngsters, Lloyd Irving, sixteen, and Bert Galbreath, seventeen, confessed to police that they killed Edward Glenn, a white man, on the night before the fight. Glenn and A. W. Watson, both teamsters, had fought the teens at midnight in the downtown. Glenn died of a fractured skull, the result of a brick thrown by Galbreath. The fracas between the four started over an argument about who might win the fight, Watson told police. Watson said he and Glenn had boasted that Flynn "would knock that nigger

Johnson's block off." The black teens in a written statement said Glenn had made an insulting remark to a neighbor woman who had passed by on the street. The two youngsters were arrested early in the morning of July the Fourth.[2]

In Columbus, Ohio, on July 5, celebrating the victory of Johnson over Flynn, an unknown black man shot three white men, following an argument that had to do with the fight's outcome. A mob gathered, but the black man escaped in the confusion.[3]

In Little Rock, Arkansas, John Williams, a black man, was lynched by a mob at nearby Plumerville on July 5.[4] Williams reportedly had killed Special Deputy Paul Nisler when officers attempted to break up a brawl during a picnic in a black community. The turmoil may have involved the prizefight of Johnson and Flynn, police said.

To no one's surprise, Chicago celebrated Johnson's victory without any unfortunate occurrences. News that Jack Johnson had vanquished Jim Flynn in New Mexico was the signal for the beginning of a celebration by hundreds of African Americans near the champion's home. The delirium of joy gained such momentum that a riot call was sent to the police, and the African Americans who had begun a parade through the streets were rerouted by a small army of bluecoats. One of the revelers grew enthusiastic enough to fire a pistol several times in the street. He was promptly arrested.

The first news flash announcing that Jack Johnson had won in nine rounds was the signal for the beginning of a celebration that gathered in size like a hardened snowball rolling down a hill on a windy day.

From 5:00 to 6:00 p.m. on Independence Day, Chicago's "Black Belt," located at Thirty-First Street and State Street, was filled with nothing but joy.[5] Returns of the fight were received in every café, show house, and saloon in the district, which accounted for the fact that everyone, apparently, learned of Johnson's triumph at the same time.

Out into State Street poured citizens, all of one color. From Dearborn Street and Armour Avenue they came also, the latter crowd the most demonstrative of them all. Because State Street at Thirty-First Street fairly swarmed with Johnson admirers, an impromptu parade was quickly organized. Automobiles, taxis, and even wagons were pressed into service.

Those who could find nothing to ride marched on foot. Conspicuous among the latter was a black man carrying a curtain pole to which he had attached a frying pan and a side of bacon, typifying "bringing home the bacon."

Mrs. Tiny Johnson, the champion's mother, and some near relatives of the fighter received news of Johnson's victory while attending the Grand Theater at Thirty-First Street and State Street. Before the result came in, pictures showing Johnson and Flynn preparing for the battle were shown on the screen. Hundreds of African Americans celebrated in the neighborhood of Johnson's home.

"Well, white folks, how did you like the Flynn-Johnson fight?" is how a black man named Nelson Jones addressed Frank Hopkins and Otis Gruell, both of them white, at Russell Avenue and Pike Street, in Covington, Kentucky. According to police, there was no immediate reply from the white men.[6]

Suddenly, one of the white men landed a Johnson-like blow on the chin of one of the black men. That caused him to topple through a large pane of glass and suffer a severe cut on one arm.

Covington patrolman Schneider heard the crashing of the glass and took the black man and the two white men to jail, charging all three with disorderly conduct. There was no other trouble of that kind in Covington.

A death occurred in Denver, but not from racial turbulence. Henry McHenry, a flagman for the Colorado and Southern Railroad, died from extreme agitation of the heart while talking with a fellow worker about what might happen on the Fourth of July in Las Vegas. McHenry was on duty at Third and Larimer Streets at the time he was stricken. By the time the police ambulance arrived, McHenry was dead. He was sixty-five years old and he left a family.[7]

The fight outcome that spurred both anger and celebration was not immediately known by everyone, of course. Communication in 1912 was simply nowhere near what it is today. A century ago, newspapers and printed matter took time to reach the public. Radio broadcasts weren't heard until 1920.

Coming to the rescue of boxing fans nationwide were street-corner heralds, men who shouted out the reports through the afternoon. For example, Horace E. Sherman stood in front of the *Albuquerque Morning Journal* and gave listeners the news from Las Vegas. It helped that Sherman had a powerful voice.

Meanwhile, inside the *Morning Journal* office building, a switchboard stayed busy with telephone calls from interested fans who requested updates.[8]

In Pueblo, Colorado, Jim Flynn's hometown, fight fans were encouraged to telephone the *Star-Journal* newspaper, which received full reports of the fight from an Associated Press wire, as did many newspapers. Employees at the *Chieftain*, Pueblo's other newspaper, mounted a giant megaphone in an upstairs window of the newspaper to let the milling crowd below know how the clash was going. Cheers rose up in the third round when fans heard that Flynn had left the champion with a small nick on his face.

CHAPTER 29

The Rewards of an Ugly Afternoon

SHORTLY BEFORE THE prizefight began, members of several Chicago homing-pigeon clubs got together and shipped eighteen pigeons to Las Vegas. The birds would be used for liberation from the arena immediately following the bout. The Chicagoans believed that the pigeons might set a distance record and bring a sense of peace and gladness to the event.

Those club members in Chicago did not know that pigeons had already gathered in the Las Vegas arena. Not homing pigeons, but ticket buyers who fell for one of the greatest cons in fistiana's long history.

So unsavory was the New Mexico presentation that the late Marquess of Queensbury, who in 1865 created an honor code for boxing matches, undoubtedly would have wept at the sight.

Reactions to the fight by those who witnessed it bordered on revulsion more than anything else. Blame for the foozle went to just about everyone. Ed Smith, the referee, let head-butting, mostly by Flynn with his forehead, go on and on, even after several warnings. Yet when the fight was done, Smith, seemingly forgetful of his admonitions to the Fireman, said, "Jim Flynn disgraced everybody."

Jack Johnson, who dallied with Flynn throughout, exhibited one of the oldest ring dodges known. Throughout the fight he would grasp Flynn's arm or shoulder with one hand and jerk him forward as he planted with the other hand a solid uppercut to the Fireman's skull.

Not for one moment was the fight a thing of beauty. Ed Smith, supposedly the ringmaster, was there to keep order. Instead, he looked the other way as Johnson and Flynn clinched regularly, then lumbered together across the canvas like a couple of capering elephants caught up in a hug fest.

Flynn rushed directly at Johnson in the ring when he had told the public that he would not do so. He said he would let Johnson carry the fight to him. The head-butting he had learned from Tommy Ryan, who knew enough to be absent from this unbecoming engagement. And then there was Captain Fred Fornoff and his New Mexico Mounted Police. A prize-fight is supposed be three men in the ring. Suddenly, there were six uniformed men in the Las Vegas arena. Fornoff said later, "I stopped the fight when it ceased to be a contest. Flynn was covered with blood and he had no chance to win."

Flynn and Johnson each said they would have kept going had it not been for Fornoff. This was a heavyweight boxing championship, after all, not a quilting bee. How badly was Flynn hurt? On July 5, the *St. Louis Post-Dispatch* provided a medical report:

One split nose
One flattened nose
One cut eye
One deviated septum
One cauliflower aural and adornment
One absolute drubbing

Here is the medical report on Johnson:

One tiny blister on his lower lip, the gift from a Flynn head-butt

Back in January, Flynn had agreed to take on Johnson gratis. However, when the fight ended, Curley, clearly feeling sorry for the Fireman, asked friends for donations to help the challenger. When all was said and done, Flynn returned to Colorado with $6,000 in cash in his pockets. Curley also saw to it that Flynn receive an automobile for his labors in the ring. Not a new automobile but *a secondhand one!* A used motor car in exchange for a battered kisser.

The attendance figure was said to be fewer than four thousand, down from an expected high of ten thousand. Some months before, seventeen thousand fans had been expected.

The extremely poor gate did not match the fight's expenses. The pathetic attendance explains why there was so little money left in the coffers. Curley surely worried about finances.[1]

For the previous night's match, which Johnson had attended, two young boxers had drawn three thousand fans to the arena. The two men had been promised 50 percent of the turnout, which amounted to $2,000. Curley would only give them a couple of hundred dollars each. When the young fighters complained, Curley's hired hands threatened them and the boxers returned to Albuquerque without staying for the Johnson-Flynn contest. Mark Levy, who promoted that fight, eventually returned what was due the two.

Not only was the main attraction of low quality, but no one made currency except Johnson, who did well. He claimed $5,000 betting on himself and $31,000 that Curley paid him. Etta also won a pile of cash by betting on her husband.[2]

Several newspapers disregarded the fight or simply buried it. The *Tacoma Daily Ledger* in Washington, for example, did not put the outcome on page one. Instead, the story was banished to page five. The Wolgast-Rivers light-weight battle made the front page.

Few newspapers agreed with Fornoff's decision to halt the fight. One of the most vitriolic responses to the fight came from Chicago reporter John I. Day, always a provocateur. Incensed by the outcome of the fight, Day sarcastically referred in print to Fornoff as "Fernoff," and accused him of grandstanding and four-flushing. Day saved his nastiest polemic for a physical description of Captain Fornoff: "A bullnecked, melon-headed, cowbellied backwoodsman parading the power of which he has been clothed by political appointments."

Unable to restrain himself, Day added further touches: "More than any thought of law and order undoubtedly was behind this over-fed, ponderous person, when he stepped into the picture. There was no arguing with the chief and his lieutenants when they demanded a halt and hands-up because Captain Fernoff is the head of a bunch of fun men as ever packed a Colt. A prison record is no bar to service on this force."

An hour or so after the fight finished, Flynn wired his mother in Pueblo. Delusional as always, he said, "Never felt better. Only injury is a cut on the nose." To the bitter conclusion, Flynn believed he was unhurt. In fact, he said he was "whipping Johnson" at the fight's completion.[3]

Not surprisingly, Flynn went for the race card when he contacted his mother. "They (people of New Mexico) don't know anything about fighting in this country of greasers. And that's why they stole the fight from me."

The consensus was that the champion could have won any time he wished. Johnson told a reporter that Flynn never hurt him at all. Flynn told another reporter that he had been robbed of a victory. Humiliation seemed to follow Flynn.

The morning after this bust, businessman F. B. Ufer of Tulsa, Oklahoma, filed a writ of attachment against Flynn. Ufer claimed that Flynn had borrowed a few hundred dollars from him some time before and refused to pay it back. O'Malley, Curley, and the First National Bank were included in the action.

On his way back to Colorado in his preowned car, with his girlfriend, Fannie Vedder, beside him, Flynn stopped in Trinidad.[4] A reporter for the Trinidad newspaper told Flynn that he "looked the worse for wear." Flynn did not say anything. The reporter wrote, "He was in no frame of mind to discuss one of the poorest exhibitions in the history of the ring."

When he reached Pueblo, Flynn told his many fans that he was forced to launch head-butts because of Johnson's holding. Many in Pueblo agreed, even those who had not witnessed the fight. Though Flynn had lost, a banquet for him was already being organized. It would take place in Pueblo, the date not clear.

Meanwhile, C. W. Patrick, Flynn's staunchest ally, attempted to scrounge up evidence to prove that Flynn had defeated Johnson. Finding such information must have been difficult. Patrick did discover that the *Omaha Bee* was claiming Flynn to be champion, as was the *Cincinnati Enquirer*, which strangely said that Flynn was "refereed out of the fight." A headline in the *Atlanta Journal* offered this blunt appraisal of the affair: "Jim Flynn Is Slaughtered."

Arthur Greiner, a member of the Flynn camp, declared that the fight lost $20,000 and perhaps more. Greiner, whose role in Las Vegas was a sinecure, said Flynn had wrecked chances of getting people to Las Vegas by ruining the moving pictures that were taken, and with his foul tactics.

"Flynn had a chance to make good," Greiner went on. "He did not prove equal to the occasion in any area. The pictures were the only chance we had to get even. Flynn acted the part of an ingrate, while Johnson acted the part of a gentleman."

When the fight concluded, H. W. Lanigan attempted to keep a low profile. However, on July 10, the *Las Vegas Optic* ran the following bizarre item: "Mr. Lanigan wishes to deny the statement given out by Mr. Johnson that people sitting at ringside shouted for Mr. Flynn to bite."

"Mr. Lanigan's version of the incident was that some people at ringside shouted for Mr. Flynn to butt."

George T. Pardy, a sporting writer from Chicago, said that the crowd, which he called "boobs," had been misled for months by an unscrupulous press agent. That would be Lanigan again, of course.

Johnson and his wife left Las Vegas only hours after the nonsense had ceased. Poor Etta. She was more troubled than anyone knew. On the train trip back to Chicago, she attempted to take her life by climbing out a window of the couple's Pullman stateroom. Johnson managed to tug her back safely into their train car.

At almost every stop Johnson's postfight train made, the champion was met with large receptions. At Emporia, Kansas, 1,500 people stood on the platform waiting for Johnson in a rainstorm. At Dodge City, Kansas, a large group of fans crowded near the windows of the train's dining car to watch Johnson eat breakfast. At Hutchinson, Kansas, a large delegation of African Americans, three thousand strong in fact, greeted Johnson with loud cheers and great applause.

The champion made a speech in Hutchinson. "Ladies and Gentlemen, it does my hearing good to get this ovation. I beat Flynn easily. It was absolutely easier than when I whipped him in 1907."

During stops in Topeka and Kansas City, jubilation welcomed the champion. In Chicago, the train's last stop, Johnson told thousands that Flynn should have been disqualified early in the fight. Another reception met him at his residence on the South Side. As soon as he had told his mother and friends there about the fight, he jumped in his racing car and buzzed around town.

The Café de Champion, Johnson's nightclub, formally opened on July 11. It was truly a posh expanse. For the convenience of expectorating patrons, Johnson had purchased cuspidors bearing his own monogram. The spittoons cost $67.50 each. Paintings in the café's "entertainment room," which could seat five hundred people comfortably, cost $15,000. The silver water pitcher and the silver service—which held spices, lemon peels, and coffee beans to decorate the bar—cost $3,000.

In the months following the fight, Johnson talked of fighting again. He also spoke of retiring. He went back and forth. Barely two months after the fight, Etta Johnson took her life with a pistol in the bedroom they shared. Johnson had already been seeing another white woman in Chicago. He had gone out that night to pick up train tickets for Etta, but he rushed home when he heard the news. Etta had been feeling fine and, curiously, had planned to return to Las Vegas with Ed Smith's wife, Sedan Smith.

In Las Vegas, Sedan Smith had become close to Etta. The two women may have been looking for a certain comfort together there. For Mrs. Smith, Las Vegas represented sadness because of her son's death there. Some say that Etta was going there to establish residence and obtain a divorce by mutual agreement.

Strangely, the word went out that some citizens in Las Vegas wanted another fight in the community, hard as that might be to understand. Charles O'Malley, it was believed, would do the staging of this meet-up, assisted by local men who had lost money in the July Fourth travesty.[5]

Their idea was to take a chance this time on making a match a success and thus getting back money they had lost on the Johnson-Flynn travesty. "There would be no outside promoter, or even promoters," the *Albuquerque Morning Journal* reported.

The Morning Journal and the *Las Vegas Optic* had been at odds ever since it was announced that the fight would come to New Mexico. In its editorials the *Morning Journal* took every opportunity to criticize the Las Vegas newspaper for sloppy reporting, and called the *Optic* the "Floptic." In return, the *Optic* accused the *Morning Journal* of being jealous because the city had failed to obtain the fight.

The *Optic* certainly did some strange things. Instead of issuing a complete rundown on a world championship the day afterward, the newspaper published a three-thousand-word screed written by Norman Skinner, a local Presbyterian minister.[6] The essay began with a few brief sentences that barely touched on the fight. The remainder was an agonizingly drawn out and puzzling labor of pomposity. It attempted to make a parallel between Pontius Pilate and Governor William C. McDonald.

To almost everyone's utter astonishment, only one week after the dust settled in Las Vegas, Charles O'Malley showed interest in putting together another bout in the town.

CHAPTER 30

Final Gong

IN SPITE OF the many storms he faced in his life—a prison sentence, female troubles, deaths of loved ones, and racial unrest—Jack Johnson managed to live to age sixty-eight. He died June 10, 1946, from injuries he suffered in an automobile accident in North Carolina.

Johnson had been en route to New York from Texas, where he had recently concluded a personal-appearance tour. There he had answered questions about his boxing career and talked about whatever else came into his head.

In the car also was Fred L. Scott, a friend who went on the trip with Johnson to share the driving of a 1939 Lincoln Zephyr. The two men had left New York on May 23 and arrived in Lufkin, Texas, on May 27.[1] Scott said that Johnson required a companion because his hearing and memory were impaired. Scott was paid twenty-five dollars a week and Johnson took care of all travel expenses. The two men had gotten to know each other in the Manhattan hotel where both were staying.

At noon on June 10, the Zephyr stopped at a diner in the Raleigh area. There has long existed a story that Johnson and Scott were refused service and told they had to eat out on the back stoop. "We were hungry," Scott told police, "and the food had already been served, so we ate. But back in the car, Jack really got angry," Scott said.

"He put the pedal down and was soon going better than seventy miles per hour."

According to Scott, who survived the accident, the men were approaching tiny Franklinton, North Carolina, on US Highway 1.

Witnesses said Johnson was barreling along at a very high rate of speed. Suddenly Johnson lost control of the wheel as a truck was approaching on a curve. To avoid the truck, Johnson pulled the car to the right, and slammed into a light pole.

Scott received a sprained left knee and lacerations of the mouth when thrown from the car.[2] Johnson was taken to Saint Agnes Hospital in Raleigh, where he died from profound shock, three fractured ribs on his left side, a dislocated hip, and multiple lacerations about his extremities, as well as internal injuries. He was declared dead at 6:10 p.m.[3]

The last twenty-two years of Johnson's life had been placid ones. He peddled whiskey, led an orchestra, opened a gym in New York City, carried a spear in a production of *Aida*, and gave lectures for a dime to small audiences who struggled to remember who he was. To the end, this one-time emperor still wore the snazziest of clothes.

Johnson was buried in Chicago's Graceland Cemetery. No boxers attended his funeral or sent a floral wreath. He lies alongside the second of his wives, Etta Terry Duryea Johnson, who had accompanied him to Las Vegas.[4]

Over the years, several people, including Senator John McCain, who had boxed during his time at the US Naval Academy, sought to get Johnson pardoned. But nothing came of those proposals. On May 18, 2018, in a quirky ceremony in the Oval Office, President Donald Trump, at the urging of actor Sylvester Stallone, the star of five *Rocky* movies, issued a posthumous pardon of Johnson.

It did not seem to matter that Trump clearly did not know much about Jack Johnson, or Rambo for that matter. A staffer likely told the president that Johnson had been imprisoned for "a racially motivated injustice." That would be the little-used Mann Act, created in 1910 to outlaw white-slave trafficking across state lines for immoral purposes. With the stroke of a pen, the ten months Johnson spent in a friendly hoosegow long ago would now be erased.

After his second fight with Johnson, Jim Flynn went on to claim a dash of fame in the ring. On February 13, 1917, the Fireman knocked out Jack Dempsey in Murray, Utah. In fact, Flynn flattened Dempsey within two minutes of the first round. Dempsey said he had neglected to warm up properly and earlier had hurt one of his hands in, of all places, a bowling alley.[5]

In a rematch on February 14, 1918, in Fort Sheridan, Wyoming, Dempsey hammered Flynn senseless in the opening round. Their first fight was the only occasion during Dempsey's fifteen years of competitive boxing when anyone knocked him out.

Following the Las Vegas bout, Flynn settled in his Colorado hometown where he remained a popular luminary. He eventually left Pueblo for good in 1921 when the Arkansas River flooded its banks and caused great devastation. Fifteen hundred people were killed and more than $20 million in damages was incurred.

For a while, Flynn put down roots in Mexico, and then relocated to Phoenix. On funds he obtained in a benefit bout in Arizona, he set himself up with a cabstand and drove a taxi. After a time, he moved on from Phoenix and took up residence in the Los Angeles area. There he gained nonspeaking roles in a few Hollywood motion pictures, usually acting as a fight trainer or sparring partner.

Flynn married Fanny Vedder, who attended the fight in Las Vegas. Coincidently, she later moved to Hoboken, New Jersey, Flynn's birthplace.

In Los Angeles, Flynn ran a bar for a spell and later a café on Third and Main Streets. Money troubles kept him from keeping either business. On April 6, 1933, celebrities of the sports world (boxer Billy Papke) and the entertainment stage (singer Al Jolson) gathered at the Pasadena Arena to hold a benefit for the destitute Flynn. A heart attack ultimately claimed Flynn on April 12, 1935. "Jim Flynn Takes Count," said his obituary in the *Los Angeles Times*.[6]

Born on Christmas Eve, he died at age fifty-five, two days before Palm Sunday. It is doubtful Flynn had been inside a church in many years. Flynn never won a championship when he was fighting. Even so, he was a fearless competitor who would pit himself against anyone.

The *Pueblo Chieftain* on April 13, 1935, remembered Flynn this way: "A portion of fame and hero worship were his for a brief period during his heyday. Then the advance of age cut him off in the only sure means of livelihood he knew. His last years were in glaring contrast to the early times of plenty."[7]

George A. Newton, sports editor of the *Chieftain*, recalled, "He was of the type worshipped by fans—a type that will fight a panther and give the cat the first two bites." Flynn's style, said Newton, reflected the rough-and-tumble, free-for-all fracases with guys in steel mills, warehouses, and brickyards.

Flynn's last words came with a smile and this gasp, "I'm groggy, but I'm not out. You won't have to throw in the towel." He is buried in Cavalry Catholic Cemetery in East Los Angeles.

When the Las Vegas fight ended, Harold W. Lanigan returned to Hot

Springs, Arkansas, to continue handling public relations for the local racetrack and luxury hotels. He stayed busy there for part of the year through 1915, alternately working on staff for a couple of publications in New York City.

Lanigan clearly had missed newspapering, because for the next four years he wrote sports for the *Boston American*. He then bounced around, as newsmen did in that era. He put in time with the *New York Daily News* and then became night editor for the Hearst News wire service in Manhattan. He went from there to the copy desk at the *Syracuse American*. That stint was followed by a return to the Hearst News service, this time in its Newark office. He finished up at the *New York American*, where he was assistant night editor.

In the 1940s, Lanigan moved to Florida where he retired. He died December 14, 1948, in New Port Richey, Florida. He was seventy-four.

Ed Smith, the referee for the 1912 fight, and a longtime Chicago newspaperman, died of a stroke in California's Hollywood Hospital on February 23, 1936. He was sixty-seven.[8]

Smith worked for several Chicago newspapers in the days celebrated in the play and film *The Front Page*. It was while writing for the *Chicago American*, from 1907 to 1926, that he gained a national reputation for his sports columns. In 1927, Smith moved to California for health reasons.

The byline "Ed W. Smith" was known across the country. Settling in the West, Smith worked a spell for the *Los Angeles Examiner*. He had suffered an initial stroke in Chicago and that caused him to walk with a cane for the remainder of his life.

In spite of his failure to disqualify Flynn during the Las Vegas fight, Smith was recognized as a respectable referee. He had officiated the famed Hackenschmidt-Gotch wrestling match and a few hundred other contests in Chicago. After World War I, he experienced heart trouble and that eventually sent him to California where he died. On his second day in Hollywood Hospital, he fell out of bed and suffered a broken collarbone.

"Looks like they're really out to get me this time, doesn't it?" he joked to friends. "Death Wins Last Round," the *Examiner* story said. In Chicago he had gained the reputation of "If Ed Smith says so, it's so." He was no longer smoking cigars in his last days, and had switched to a pipe.

Jack Curley, the promoter of the 1912 fight, died of a heart attack in Great Neck, Long Island, New York, on June 12, 1937. He was buried at Nassau Knolls, Port Washington, New York. He was sixty-one.[9]

Curley had stepped away from boxing following the Johnson-Willard bout in 1915. Yet he stayed busy by becoming one of the most versatile and industrious promoters ever. He mainly advanced wrestling matches, a sport which then was taken seriously. Today, professional wrestling is all about clowning, wild costumes, throwing chairs, and various forms of horseplay.

Curley's promotional skills led to a wide range of events. For instance, he signed William Jennings Bryan to do a lecture tour, convinced Rudolph Valentino to make a series of personal appearances, and backed Barney Oldfield in several car races. He sponsored Enrico Caruso in numerous concerts and signed on Bill Tilden to play in various tennis matches.

It was in securing wrestling bouts that Curley truly shined. He brought wrestling into the golden era of sport and pyramided the public's foolability into a fortune. And even when the customers were told plainly and pointedly that these matches, with championships involved, were prearranged, rehearsed, and strictly burlesqued, they still paid off in terms of money. One match that Curley set up drew $75,000 in New York, between two combatants who had previously wrestled each other sixty-eight times.

Not only was Curley talented, he was an imaginative and adventuresome promoter, the likes of which disappeared long ago.

Curley eventually divorced Marie Drescher, the young woman he wed in Las Vegas and with whom he fathered two children.

William Calhoun McDonald, the first statehood governor of New Mexico, and a man who put the fight on hold for five months, died of Bright's disease, a kidney disorder known today as nephritis. His passing came April 11, 1918, in an El Paso, Texas, hospital. He was fifty-nine.

McDonald's waffling on the prizefight issue cast a long shadow nationwide. He caused the contest to be a question mark for scores of boxing fans not just in New Mexico but everywhere. To some voters, the governor's indecisiveness may have hindered the plans of those who had considered attending the bout.

McDonald's death for many was unexpected. In fact, numerous New Mexico officials thought the former governor was in reasonably good health. Intimates, however, knew he had been failing slowly. In March 1918, McDonald attended a gathering held at the Alvarado Hotel in Albuquerque. In what seemed a casual manner, he remarked briefly to a friend, "I think I better go home and straighten up my affairs for I have not long to live."

When McDonald left the Alvarado that day, he went directly to his ranch north of Carrizozo, New Mexico. On April 12, he announced he was going to receive treatment in Texas. His family argued against that, possibly suspecting he would die there and not at his beloved ranch.

Stubborn as always, McDonald reached El Paso by train. He walked directly from the station to the Hotel Dieu, a hospital opened by four sisters of the Daughters of Charity in 1894. It was named after the famous Hotel Dieu in Paris.

It is not clear why he went to that hospital, though McDonald had a strong religious faith. It's likely he prayed about such a decision. His wife and their son-in-law, T. A. Spencer, were at his bedside when he died. He would have been sixty years old that July. He was buried in Cedarvale Cemetery in White Oaks, New Mexico.

There remained one more bungling with ties to the Johnson-Flynn fight. The dates of Governor McDonald's administration were wrongly inscribed on the top of McDonald's headstone. The marker reads "1911–1915" when it should read "1912–1917."

Obituaries were mostly kind to McDonald, but some called him "uncompromising and cautious." Nowhere were those characteristics seen more than in the weeks leading up to the Las Vegas fight. He went from expressing genuine interest in having the fight in New Mexico to believing the fight would attract all number of bad eggs. It is possible that his delayed decision on the prizefight may have caused some voters to not reelect him as governor. In fact, McDonald's foot-dragging followed him to 1916, when he failed in a bid to become lieutenant governor. Indeed, he had enemies even within his own party.

Not one obituary mentioned McDonald's role in the Johnson-Flynn farce.

An editorial in the *Albuquerque Morning Journal* after his death said, "Naturally when a man goes into politics, he makes enemies. Governor McDonald was no exception to this rule. There were men in his own party who found fault with many of his political doings. Even so, McDonald gave the state a clean businesslike administration."

McDonald wasn't completely forgotten. His death led a group of farmers and oilmen in Lea County, just north of Lovington, to name their unincorporated community McDonald. Soon McDonald, New Mexico, had its own post office. That building stood until August 2010. This little crossroads in southeast New Mexico, population thirty, still has its own zip code: 88262.[10]

The end for Captain Fred Fornoff, the New Mexico Mounted Police officer who climbed into the ring to stop the fight in the midst of the final round, came on November 26, 1935. Fornoff died in Wyoming, at a US military hospital at Fort Sheridan. He was seventy-six. His health had begun to fail eight years before, at which time he was hospitalized. He was buried in the National Cemetery in Santa Fe, New Mexico.[11]

Fornoff served four different governors and led his band of men in wiping out lawlessness, especially cattle thievery. From 1913 to 1918, only one mounted policeman in New Mexico existed—Fred Fornoff. He took a good deal of criticism and ridicule for halting the fight, most of it from the Flynn camp and the press. However, Fornoff stood by his actions that July the Fourth, 1912. He never apologized and never said later that he would have done things differently.

Arthur W. Greiner, a Curley confidant and gofer in Las Vegas, died May 25, 1917, in a Milwaukee sanitarium. Greiner was thirty-three. He reportedly had been seriously ill for several months, following a nervous breakdown. The collapse came when he and Mrs. Greiner were living at Chicago's Edgewater Beach Hotel. In the hope of recovering his health, relatives had him relocated to a sanitarium, but there his health sank gradually.[12]

It's not clear whether Greiner's breakdown had been caused by the death of his mechanic, Sam Dickson, at the first Indianapolis 500. However, Greiner's carelessness in that race definitely was a factor in Dickson's death.

In the five years following that Indianapolis 500, Greiner got divorced, remarried, divorced again, and remarried once more. All his wives were showgirls.

Following his prizefight years, Tommy Cannon, the ring announcer in Las Vegas, decided to settle down with his wife and children in Shawnee, Oklahoma, in Indian Territory. There he worked as keeper for a steam railroad and as a merchant in a feed store. He died in Shawnee in 1933. He was seventy-four years old.

Charles Francis O'Malley, point man in bringing the fight to Las Vegas, died in a hospital there on October 16, 1969, after a brief illness. His body was taken to Fairview Memorial Park, Albuquerque, for cremation. O'Malley was eighty-two.

To no one's surprise, O'Malley's obituary made the front page of the *Las Vegas Optic*. He took to his grave that he had played major-league baseball for four years. It was never questioned by anyone in Las Vegas.

"Charles O'Malley Services Held Sunday at St. Paul's Church": *Las Vegas Optic*, October 20, 1969.

Each year, as grand marshal, O'Malley directed and led the Cowboy Reunion's parade on horseback. In 1958, much against his will, his horse was replaced by a Jeep. Active in Rotary, O'Malley for a decade was the chief of the East Las Vegas Fire Department. At the time of his death, he was made an honorary member. Why he fabricated a career in professional baseball is not known. Perhaps he wanted to believe that tale because he so badly yearned to land a world championship prizefight in little Las Vegas. As bizarre as that event turned out, it put New Mexico on the map for half a dozen slapstick months.

ACKNOWLEDGMENTS

Many thanks to Clark Whitehorn, former executive editor of the University of New Mexico Press. Clark was acutely aware of New Mexico's deeply ingrained boxing culture and history. That said, he believed strongly in this project early on. From the beginning, Clark offered needed guidance, supportive advice, and valued suggestions. His unwavering patience in me is greatly appreciated.

Several people helped to put together *Crazy Fourth* and each deserves a special thanks.

Stephen Hull, director of the University of New Mexico Press, saw a necessary need for this story and pushed for it to be published.

Sonia Dickey, acquisitions editor with the University of New Mexico Press, answered many of my questions and offered instructions several steps along the way.

Kirk Perry lent a thorough, thoughtful, and astute hand in the copyediting of the manuscript.

Daniel Kosharek and Hannah Abelbeck, photo imaging specialists at the New Mexico History Museum in the Palace of the Governors, Santa Fe, and Michael Rebman, the museum overseer and photo-imaging specialist at the City of Las Vegas Rough Rider Museum, Las Vegas, New Mexico, helped to locate images for *Crazy Fourth*.

The *Albuquerque Journal* provided me space to publish my first boxing efforts. When I joined the *Journal*'s sports department, Mike Hall, then supervisor of that section of the newspaper, pointed me to a desk directly behind one occupied by Rick Wright. Rick gracefully and prescriptively covered boxing for the *Journal*. The position of my desk proved consequential. If you wanted to learn about boxing, and I did, and wished to describe it for *Journal* readers, which I also desired to do, you took a back seat to Rick.

Johnny Tapia supplied me with story after story. Rick wrote a lot about

Tapia's fine amateur boxing career. In 1988, Tapia blazed onto the professional fight scene, having then only a single tattoo and an undefeated record. He had the world in his pocket, it appeared. In 1990, I finally gained an interview with Tapia, who had recently turned pro. I remember sitting in my car with him at a Sonic Drive-In on South Broadway in Albuquerque, near the gym where he trained. Tapia sniffled during much of our conversation. Got a cold, he said. No reason for me to question that. A week or so on, Tapia tested positive for cocaine and was suspended from boxing for three and a half years. Those were hard years for Tapia, who some nights slept beneath bridges.

They were difficult times too for an Albuquerque sports writer who suddenly lacked a charismatic subject. When Tapia came back, I managed to report on a couple of his fights when Rick Wright was busy with other matters. In time, I wrote about the murder of Tapia's mother, an act that surely fueled his rage in the ring and perhaps explained his untamed life out of it. I wrote about Wells Park, the Albuquerque neighborhood that Tapia knew best. I wrote about his intense rivalry with Danny Romero, a fighter raised just a few blocks away from where Tapia grew up.

Thanks to those who helped make Johnny Tapia and Jack Johnson larger-than-life figures, though Johnson at 220 pounds was physically far larger. Both boxers had admirers and detractors. I must admit that at times I vacillated between the two factions, admiring Tapia one moment then being appalled by his behavior the next. The two men possessed insatiable desires. For Johnson, it was women. For Tapia, white powder. Both spent almost a year in prison. Like Johnson, Tapia fought once as a professional in Las Vegas, New Mexico (only to lose). Each fighter continued to step inside the ropes long past his prime.

In 2011, I reported on Tapia's final bout, held at Isleta Casino. Two years after that, I attended a teary memorial for him, held on the floor of a mobbed University of New Mexico basketball arena. Like many people, I knew that day would come, though I had hoped Johnny might reach fifty years. Five years short of that, Mi Vida Loca's heart gave out.

Tapia more than once shared with me his admiration for Jack Johnson, whom he had scrutinized on YouTube. Thus, it is not surprising that both men acted similarly in a boxing ring. They frequently talked to, grinned at, and snickered in the direction of spectators in their seats and at opponents

in front of them. Their curious likenesses are why I dedicated this book to
Tapia. Troubled as Johnny was, I miss the guy.

Susan Keil Smith—a wonderful companion to have on research trips to
Las Vegas, New Mexico, as well as to Denver and Pueblo, Colorado, and to
New York City—more than anyone, listened to my thoughts about the man-
uscript and encouraged me to complete it.

Jedediah Smith spent the better part of a day digging up valuable material
inside the Chicago Historical Library.

Carson Smith gave able assistance in many areas, prowling the shelves of
Powell's Books in Portland, Oregon, for hard-to-find works about Jack Johnson, and providing his computer wizardry. Carson has followed boxing since
boyhood. As a college student, he reported for the *Roundup*, the student
newspaper at New Mexico State University. In May 2000, he interviewed
Johnny Tapia who had come to Las Cruces for a fight in the Pan American
Center, where he won on a unanimous decision.

The interlibrary loan system is a bountiful gift for a nonfiction writer
tasked with combing material from more than a century gone by. The ILL
department at the University of New Mexico and the ILL desk at the Albuquerque Public Library retrieved for me rolls and rolls of microfilm from several dozen newspapers across the country, particularly those from 1912. The
ILL staffs at both places also came forth with hard-to-find copies of magazines
and a wide range of books, not just about boxing but about race, culture, and
life in America more than a hundred years ago.

Anyone who attempts to write about Johnson cannot do so without a
close reading of Geoffrey C. Ward's distinguished *Unforgiveable Blackness:
The Rise and Fall of Jack Johnson*. The same goes for Randy Roberts's thoroughly engaging *Papa Jack: Jack Johnson and the Era of White Hopes*.

Chris Cozzone's fascinating *Boxing in New Mexico, 1868–1940* makes sure
to give full due to the Johnson-Flynn affair, and does so in lively and clear
prose, with a keen eye for details.

Raymond Wilson's article about the fight—so simple yet so straightfor-
ward—found a home in three different publications, as well as in this one.

Many specific librarians offered assistance: Jan Perone, newspaper librar-
ian for the Abraham Lincoln Presidential Library, Springfield, Illinois; Den-
nis Daily, Special Collections, Pikes Peak Library District, Colorado Springs,
Colorado; Mallory Pillard, Carnegie Public Library, Trinidad, Colorado;

Aaron Ramirez, Special Collections, Rawlings Library, Pueblo, Colorado; Jessica Archuleta, Pueblo City-County Library District, Rawlings Branch, Pueblo, Colorado; and Cyndie Harlan, director, Hearst Library, Lead, South Dakota.

Barbara A. Klug and Jeff Rosales, though not librarians, spent a good amount of time in the Minnesota History Center where they unearthed several beneficial facts and notations.

The staffs of various libraries all deserve well-earned salutes. These include those at the Center for Southwest Research and Special Collections, Zimmerman Library, the University of New Mexico, Albuquerque; the Donnelly Library, New Mexico Highlands University, Las Vegas, New Mexico; the Western History and Genealogy Department, Denver Public Library, Denver, Colorado; the Carnegie Public Library, Las Vegas, New Mexico; the Southwest Collection, New Mexico State Library, Santa Fe, New Mexico; the Albuquerque Public Library's Special Collections branch; and the headquarters of the New York Public Library, New York, New York.

NOTES

Introduction

1. "Joe's Ringside Is Still a Good Place to Watch a Fight," *Albuquerque Journal*, June 14, 1994, C-1.

2. "Ike Davis, the Cash Grocer: The Store That's Always Open," advertisement, *Las Vegas Optic*, May 30, 1912.

3. *Las Vegas Optic*, December 30, 1957, 1.

4. Telephone conversation with Las Vegas, NM, native Ken Knoll, January 15, 2015.

5. The author caught up with Yolanda Arellanes, in Albuquerque, via a telephone conversation, June 20, 2014.

6. "Joe M. Roybal," *Las Vegas Optic*, September 6, 1993, Obituaries, 8.

7. Buckley, *But Enough About You*, 301.

8. "Jack Johnson," ESPN.com, January 24, 2001.

9. Ward, *Unforgivable Blackness*, 154–55; "That nigger can never lick me," said Jim Jeffries.

10. He was married six times. Johnson, *In the Ring—and Out*, 229; his first two wives were black women, but neither marriage lasted long. "A Pardon for Jack," *Denver Post*, November 12, 2009.

Chapter 1

1. "Jack Curley Tells How He Made the Flynn-Johnson Match," *Denver Post*, June 30, 1922, 4.

2. Hutchison, "Hyping White Hopes," 341.

3. Roberts, *Papa Jack*, 130.

4. Apparently Flynn liked to stay busy and keep his name in the newspapers. Cozzone and Boggio, *Boxing in New Mexico*, 92.

5. "He is a hard-hitter with unlimited capacity for punishment." *Denver Post*, June 30, 1911, 4.

6. "Flynn Is Violating Agreement," *Albuquerque Evening Herald*, January 15, 1912, 4.

7. "Curley Believes Flynn the Man to Whip the Negro," *Albuquerque Evening Herald*, February 26, 1912, 12.

8. "Williams Proves Easy Mark for Jim Flynn," *Albuquerque Morning Journal*, January 18, 1912, 5.

Chapter 2

1. Spink, *National Game*, 335–36.
2. "Everybody Is Coming to Las Vegas," *Las Vegas Optic*, May 1, 1912, 5.
3. "Sports Writers Register," BaseballGuru.com.
4. "Flynn 'Snapped' in Fifty Poses," *Hot Springs Sentinel-Record*, April 25, 1912, 4.
5. Greiner, twenty-seven years, was used to the good life. He briefly had been married to a sixteen-year-old actress-dancer. Leerhsen, *Blood and Smoke*, 222–23.
6. "Jack Johnson Not Badly Hurt," *Hot Springs Sentinel-Record*, April 27, 8.
7. "Flynn Was Not Allowed to Box," *Wichita Beacon*, May 4, 1912, 7.

Chapter 3

1. "Jim Flynn Makes a Prophecy," *Buffalo Enquirer*, May 8, 1912, 8.
2. "Jim Flynn in Town Says He Will Win July 4 Battle," *Colorado Springs Gazette*, May 8, 1912.
3. Breslin, *Damon Runyon: A Life*, 47–49.
4. Breslin, *Damon Runyon*, 48–49.
5. Breslin.
6. "Royal Welcome Extended Jim Flynn When He Gets Back among Home People," *Pueblo Chieftain*, May 9, 1912, 1.
7. "Flynn at the Pantages," *Pueblo Star-Journal*, 89.
8. "Flynn at Football Made Good Record," *Pueblo Chieftain*, May 9, 1912, 9. Flynn graduated from Centennial High School with the class of 1899. Telephone call by author to Centennial High School Museum, February 2, 2015.
9. "Plenty of Reasons for Picking Me Out as Winner, says Jim," *Pueblo Chieftain*, May 9, 1912.
10. "Mother Thinks Son Will Win," *Pueblo Chieftain*, May 9, 1912, 9.
11. "Flynn Makes Bank Deposit in This City," *Pueblo Chieftain*, May 9, 1912, 8.

Chapter 4

1. "States Freeze Jack Johnson," *Sporting News*, January 15, 1912, 8.
2. "Canada Wants Johnson Bout," *Santa Fe New Mexican*, January 2, 1912, 1.
3. "South Porcupine, Ontario Offers Big Prize," *Santa Fe New Mexican*, January 8, 1912, 1.
4. Curley traveled to New Mexico in April. "Jack Curley Here Today on Way to Las Vegas," *Albuquerque Evening Herald*, March 18, 1912, 18.

5. Not everyone was happy with Las Vegas's intentions to seize the fight. "Las Vegas Newspaper Out to Get Big Mill," *Albuquerque Morning Journal*, February 18, 1912.

6. "Las Vegas Bidder for Johnson-Flynn Battle," *Albuquerque Evening Herald*, January 16, 1912, 1.

7. Curley finally came to his senses in late February. "Las Vegas Chosen as Battleground; July 4 Date," *Albuquerque Morning Journal*, February 26, 1912. Curley for some reason seemed hesitant. "Promoter Curley Silent Concerning Big Fight," *Albuquerque Morning Journal*, February 4, 1912. Curley let it be known that he had selected Las Vegas, which is Spanish for "the meadows." "Las Vegas Lands Johnson-Flynn Contest," *Albuquerque Morning Journal*, April 14, 1912.

8. Arango et al., *New Mexico*, 205–6.

9. Leerhsen, *Blood and Smoke*, 219.

10. "Charles O'Malley was a freelance scout for the St. Louis Browns baseball team." Callon, *Las Vegas, New Mexico*, 280.

11. Prairie Wordsmith, https://prairiewordsmith.wordpress.com/. His obituary repeats that same information.

12. *New Mexico Business Directory, 1911–1912*, 442.

13. Bryan, *Wildest of the Wild West*, 2.

14. Bryan, 56–58.

15. Perrigo, *Gateway to Glorieta*, 44–46.

16. Perrigo, 18–19.

17. "Odd Spots and Strange People of the Southwest," *Bryan Democrat*, December 2, 1910, 1.

Chapter 5

1. "Flynn's Training Camp Invaded by Cupid," *Albuquerque Morning Journal*, May 17, 1912.

2. Steve Yohe, "A Jack Curley Bio," WrestlingClassics.com.

3. "I Wish It Were True, Is Curley's Reply," *Las Vegas Optic*, May 16, 1912.

4. "Jack Curley Weds a Pretty Denver Girl," *Las Vegas Optic*, May 22, 1912.

5. "Jack Curley's Romance Seems Slightly Tarnished," *Santa Fe New Mexican*, June 6, 1912, 2.

6. "Jack Curley Is Named in Suit for Divorce," *Albuquerque Evening Herald*, June 5, 1912, 6.

7. "Jack Curley Back from Trip to West Coast," *Albuquerque Evening Herald*, June 6, 1912, 5.

8. "Personal Mention," *Santa Fe New Mexican*, June 11, 1912, 5.

Chapter 6

1.   On May 21, Curley inspected the premises and found them ideal. He wired Johnson, telling him of the advantages of the place. "Johnson to Train at Forsyth Ranch," *Albuquerque Morning Journal*, May 22, 1912.

2.   "Johnson Threw Up His Hands in Horror," *Chicago Defender*, June 1, 1912, 6.

3.   "Jack Johnson Rejects Filthy Training Camp," *Chicago Defender*, June 1, 1912.

4.   Johnson wanted people to see him and he didn't want to be remote. "That way," he said, "there would be no stories told of me fooling away my time." Ward, *Unforgivable Blackness*, 280.

5.   "Possible Champion May Train at Jemez Springs," *Albuquerque Morning Journal*, May 26, 1912.

6.   The courting of Johnson continued. On May 28, representatives of the Albuquerque Commercial Club came to Las Vegas. The club offered the champion free quarters and the National Guard Armory as a training place. "Jack Is Popular Guy," *Milwaukee Journal*, May 29, 1912, 11.

7.   Mark Levy, the director of the New Mexico Athletic Association, kept pushing for Johnson to train in Albuquerque. Johnson held fast to the house close to the Las Vegas plaza. Johnson did promise to come to Albuquerque to put on an exhibition there in mid-June. "Johnson Refuses Albuquerque Offer," *Las Vegas Optic*, May 29, 1912.

8.   "Jack Changes Camp," *Milwaukee Journal*, May 28, 1912, 10.

Chapter 7

1.   "Elks Theater Offers the Moving Pictures of the Stars Who Meet at Las Vegas on July 4," *Santa Fe New Mexican*, May 14, 1912, 5.

2.   Wilson, "Another White Hope Bites the Dust," 33.

3.   "Johnson to Visit Santa Fe on June 7 for an Exhibition," *Albuquerque Morning Journal*, May 31, 1912.

4.   "Johnson to Box for Lawmakers," *Chicago Tribune*, June 6, 1912, 10.

5.   He would box the exhibition at 9:00 p.m. at the Elks Theatre. "The exhibition will be a clean sport and ladies need not hesitate to attend. You will not regret seeing the show." "World's Champion Here," *Santa Fe New Mexican*, June 6, 1912.

6.   "The Lord of Pugdom," a Santa Fe reporter called Johnson. The same writer said that Johnson was blessed with a grace of movement unusual in one of almost monstrous proportions and that he had an expansive smile. "Jack Johnson in Santa Fe," *Santa Fe New Mexican*, June 7, 1912, 7.

7.   "Big Smoke Makes Big Hit With Santa Feans," *Albuquerque Evening Herald*, June 7, 1912, 2.

8.   "Johnson Willing That Best Man Shall Win," *Albuquerque Morning Journal*, May 26, 1912.

9. During his lifetime, Johnson participated in seventy-eight official fights. Aside from the Jeffries bout, perhaps none compares with what took place in his hometown on February 25, 1901. Johnson and Joe Choynski met up in Galveston, Texas, in Harmony Hall, for a heavyweight match. The two heavyweights were soon arrested for violating a Texas law that prohibited prizefight contests. The pair wound up spending twenty-three days in the city jail, let out at night and returning the next morning. Ward, *Unforgivable Blackness*, 35–38. Johnson, *My Life and Battles*, 118.

10. Arango et al., *New Mexico*, 498.

11. Ward, *Unforgivable Blackness*, 280–81.

Chapter 8

1. Cannon was born in 1859. Uncle Billy Jordan was still announcing at age seventy-eight. Lang, *Nelson-Wolgast Fight*, 11.

2. "Flynn Looks Good," Lead, *South Dakota Daily Call*, June 3, 1912.

3. "Tommy Cannon Sees Both Fighters," *Kansas City Star*, May 30, 1912.

4. "Tommy Cannon Is Here," *Las Vegas Optic*, May 28, 1912.

5. "Las Vegas, Where Big Fight Will Be Held," *Cincinnati Enquirer*, May 19, 1912, section 3, 3.

6. "Listen to Tommy Cannon," *Kansas City Star*, June 7, 1912, 2B.

Chapter 9

1. "Flynn Coming to Convince Fans of Condition," *Albuquerque Morning Journal*, May 15, 1912, 6.

2. "Bill Pettus Back from Pueblo—Colored Man Who Underwent Severe Grueling at Hands of Jim Flynn," *Albuquerque Morning Journal*, Sept. 30, 1909.

3. Pettus was a baseball star. Cozzone and Boggio, *Boxing in New Mexico*, 64.

4. "Bout to Be in the Afternoon," *Chicago Daily Tribune*, June 16, 1912, 11.

5. "Flynn Will Spend Entire Day in Albuquerque," *Albuquerque Morning Journal*, May 18, 1912.

6. "The Duke City Band, headed by impresario Ben Disneo, will meet Flynn at the station. Flynn will be escorted to the Sturges Hotel where Mark Levy has engaged rooms for the party." "Flynn and Curley Will Arrive in City Tonite," *Albuquerque Morning Journal*, May 22, 1912.

7. "Numerous Fans to Greet Flynn Tonight," *Albuquerque Morning Journal*, May 23, 1912.

8. "Flynn Calls Bluff of Sheepman Last Night," *Albuquerque Morning Journal*, May 24, 1912.

9. "Flynn Showed What He Can Do with the Gloves," *Albuquerque Evening Herald*, May 24, 1912, 6.

10. "Jimmie Flynn at Orpheum Tonight," *Albuquerque Morning Journal*, May 10, 1912.

11. "Oldfield Picks Flynn to Win," *Las Vegas Optic*, May 24, 1912, 12.

Chapter 10

1. "To Start Boxing Work," *Milwaukee Journal*, June 1, 1912, 6.

2. "Plenty of Reasons for Picking Me Out as a Winner, says Jim," *Pueblo Chieftain*, May 9, 1912.

3. "Flynn Is Mistaken for Escaped Lunatic," *Las Vegas Optic*, June 3, 1912.

4. "Flynn Is Mistaken for Escaped Lunatic."

5. "Flynn Chases Chauffeur," *Chicago Evening American*, June 10, 1912.

6. Johnson, *Jack Johnson Is a Dandy*, 66.

7. "Local News," *Las Vegas Optic*, June 28, 1912, 8.

8. "Local News," 8.

9. Ward, *Unforgivable Blackness*, 280.

10. Ward, 280.

11. "Something Smells," *Chicago Evening American*, June 14, 1912, 6.

12. "Something Smells," 6.

13. "Disaster in Champ's Camp," *Los Angeles Daily Times*, July 3, 1912, part 3, 3.

14. "Disaster in Champ's Camp," part 3, 3.

15. *Evening World*, May 29, 1912, 18.

16. *Evening World*, 18.

17. *Chicago Evening American*, June 13, 1912, 12.

18. "Just a Friendly Call," *Kansas City Star*, June 6, 1912, 6.

19. "Just a Friendly Call," 6.

20. "Johnson Agrees to Fight Flynn in an Old Kind of Ring," *Albuquerque Evening Herald*, June 21, 1912, 6.

21. "Bert Smith Sees Flynn," *Los Angeles Daily Times*, June 3, 1912, part 3, 1.

22. "Bert Smith Sees Flynn," part 3, 1.

23. "Bert Smith Sees Flynn," part 3, 1.

Chapter 11

1. "Tommy Ryan Says Flynn May be Champion," *Albuquerque Evening Herald*, May 26, 1912, 6.

2. "Flynn Looks Good," *Las Vegas Optic*, June 3, 1912.

3. "Tommy Ryan Arrives at Flynn's Camp," *Buffalo Enquirer*, May 27, 1912, 8.

4. "Flynn Has Only One Style," *Chicago Evening American*, June 15, 1912.

5. "Nothing Doing at Flynn's Camp at Montezuma," *Albuquerque Evening Herald*, June 18, 1912, 6.

6. "On Tommy Ryan's Departure," *Albuquerque Morning Journal*, June 19, 1912, 6.

7. "Jim Is Fat," *Los Angeles Daily Times*, section 3, 1.

8. "Curley Discounts Rumors of Fight Being Stopped," *Albuquerque Morning Journal*, June 19, 1912, 6.

9. "Tommy Ryan Has Revenge," *Kansas City Star*, June 25, 1912, 6.

Chapter 12

1. "Big Arena Will Seat 17, 950 People," *Las Vegas Optic*, May 15, 1912.

2. "Curley Will Award Contract for Arena Early This Week," *Albuquerque Morning Journal*, May 13, 1912.

3. "Tom Flanagan in Las Vegas," *Chicago Daily Tribune*, June 22, 1912, 14.

4. "Small Ring Would Not Be a Disadvantage to Champion," *Denver Post*, June 20, 1912, 12.

5. "Ring Favors Fireman," *Milwaukee Journal*, June 22, 1912, 14.

6. Initially Curley wanted the ring to be seventeen and one half feet square, and Johnson wanted twenty-four feet. "A Squeal about the Ring," *Kansas City Star*, June 20, 1912, 10.

7. In the center of the arena stood the ring, which caused a controversy all its own. "Flanagan at Las Vegas," *Chicago Daily Tribune*, June 22, 1912, 14.

Chapter 13

1. Bryan, *Wildest of the Wild West*, 247.

2. *America's Highways 1776–1976* (Washington, DC: Federal Highway Administration, 1976).

3. "Big Day for Autoists," *Milwaukee Journal*, June 6, 1912, 8.

4. "City Notes," *Las Vegas Optic*, July 2, 1912.

5. "The Speed Germ Got Him," *Kansas City Star*, June 14, 1912, 2B.

6. "The Speed Germ Got Him," 2B.

7. Robert Edgren column, *Evening World*, June 22, 1912, 6.

8. "Johnson in City Ready to Train," *Chicago Daily Tribune*, April 29, 1912, 8.

9. The roads heading to Las Vegas presented a challenge. Some of the routes were impassable for automobiles, mostly because of weather conditions and the resulting mud. "There are not enough gasoline mechanics and mules to assist those driving. Of seven cars that left Trinidad the other day, only one got through." "Roads to Las Vegas Will Bother Autoists," *Colorado Springs Gazette*, June 30, 1912, 8.

10. Mrs. Jack Curley's automobile mishap could have been far worse. "Car Hits a Pole," *Las Vegas Optic*, June 28, 1912. "It appeared she had little practice being at the wheel. The pole was broken in two. The corner where it happened is abrupt and the

street is narrow. Mayor Lorenzo Delgado said he was going to order all street cars to sound their bells frequently as they approached the plaza. Automobiles also will be expected to make a noise to warn drivers of buggies of their approach."

11. "Sports Writers Take Plunge into Water," *Tacoma Daily Ledger*, June 29, 1912, 8.

12. "Denver Men Here after Auto Trip," *Las Vegas Optic*, June 22, 1912.

Chapter 14

1. "Thousand Negroes Plan to Descend on Meadow City," *Albuquerque Evening Herald*, June 14, 1912, 1.

2. "Many Travelers Coming," *Albuquerque Morning Journal*, May 30, 1912.

3. "Denver to Send Trainload of Fans," *Las Vegas Optic*, May 27, 1912.

4. *Albuquerque Evening Herald*, June 14, 1912, 1.

5. "Puebloans Off Tonight to Attend Big Fight," *Pueblo Chieftain*, July 3, 1912.

6. "Nelson's Obar Ranch Will Send 100 Cowboys to Ringside at Las Vegas," *St. Louis Post-Dispatch*, July 2, 1912, 15.

7. "Nelson's Obar Ranch," 15.

Chapter 15

1. "Governor Frowns upon Proposed Prize Fight," *Albuquerque Morning Journal*, February 8, 1912.

2. On June 19, McDonald's secretary, C. H. Olsen, responded personally, which he rarely did. To most letter writers, he sent off a form letter. "Others with a Form Letter," box 1, serial number 14087, State Library of New Mexico, Santa Fe, New Mexico; and William J. Downing letter, folder 27, box 1400, State Library of New Mexico.

3. From many states, the Christian Endeavor Union led the nation in condemning the fight. Eugene L. Philpot letter, folder 19, box 14100, State Library of New Mexico.

4. Some letters were simply thoughtful: C. L. Carter letter, folder 27, box 11–101, State Library of New Mexico.

5. The Laguna Indians, including their war chief, were vehemently opposed to the boxing match. In a letter to Governor McDonald, the tribe wrote, "We believe fighting to be bad and a sin. Sin is bad, whether it is big or little. Sin does not care who it hurt." "Indians Protest against Fight Scheduled for Las Vegas: Quaint Petition by Red Men of Laguna Pueblo Sent to Governor McDonald Disapproving of Johnson-Flynn Contest," *Albuquerque Morning Journal*, May 12, 1912, 1; "We the Indians of the Laguna pueblo, Valencia County, New Mexico, in meeting assembled, express our disapproval of all kinds of fighting, prizefighting or fighting for money included."

6. Frisbee, *Counterpunch*, 152. "Governor Frowns upon Proposed Prize Fight," *Albuquerque Morning Journal*, February 2, 1912.

7. "Fight Fans and Ministers at Loggerheads," *Albuquerque Morning Journal*, February 2, 1912; Cozzone and Boggio, *Boxing in New Mexico*, 139.

Chapter 16

1. "Around the State," *Santa Fe New Mexican*, June 7, 1912, 2.

2. "Official Colors of Black and White Fighters," *Albuquerque Morning Journal*, May 17, 1912.

3. "We Wish He Used Milder Language," *Santa Fe New Mexican*, June 12, 1912, 3.

4. *Pueblo Star-Journal*, July 4, 1912.

5. *Inter Ocean*, June 28, 1912, 4; *Pueblo Star-Journal*, July 4, 1912.

6. Michael Tisserand, "How a Heavyweight Champ and a Cartoonist Flouted Race Hate," *Daily Beast*, August 31, 2018.

7. Cartoon, "Dem Funny White Folks!," *Milwaukee Journal*, July 5, 1912, 11.

8. *Chicago Evening American*, June 4, 1912, 6.

9. In Tyler, Texas, two thousand people were said to have burned and then lynched a black man. "Negro Put to Death at Stake for Assault on Woman," *Albuquerque Evening Herald*, May 25, 1912, 1.

10. "Around the State," *Santa Fe New Mexican*, June 19, 1912, 2.

11. Four men were arrested and were jailed, but it was found that each could give an account of himself. Kiser was charged with inciting the recent race riot to drive African Americans from Clovis. "Around the State," *Santa Fe New Mexican*, June 19, 1912, 2.

12. *Santa Fe New Mexican*, June 21, 1912.

13. "Reports of Race Riot Greatly Exaggerated," *Clovis News*, June 13, 1912, 2; *Santa Fe New Mexican*, June 21, 1912.

14. "The Clovis Riot," *Santa Fe New Mexican*, June 19, 1912, 2.

15. "Race Riots at Cloudcroft," *Santa Fe New Mexican*, June 20, 1912.

Chapter 17

1. "Will Choose Referee," *Milwaukee Journal*, June 10, 1912, 4.

2. "Selection of Capable Man to Referee Johnson-Flynn Bout Is Important Step," *St. Louis Post-Dispatch*, June 2, 1912.

3. "Demand Is Growing That New Mexico Man Referee," *Albuquerque Morning Journal*, May 28, 1912; "Battle on Fourth May Be Refereed by Mark Levy," *Albuquerque Morning Journal*, May 1, 1912.

4. That list got shorter when Johnson scratched off the names of John Kelly and Sam Austin. Both men were from New York and Johnson had long had his

troubles with boxing officials in that city. "Doesn't Like New Yorkers," *Kansas City Star*, June 12, 2B.

5. Levy's name stayed on the list. "All of New Mexico Is Anxious to Have Him Serve," *Chicago Daily Tribune*, June 12, 1912, 15.

6. George Barton's name remained on the list of possible referees. A newspaperman from Minneapolis, with solid refereeing experience, Barton had long been a Johnson supporter. On page 45 of his autobiography, *My Lifetime in Sports*, published in 1957, Barton shed some light on why he wasn't selected to be in the ring, or sitting at ringside in July 1912.

7. There were rumors that Jim Jeffries would take the role. "I am out of the fighting game," he told a Los Angeles reporter. *Los Angeles Daily Times*, June 13, 1912, section 3. Instead, Jeffries encouraged Jack Welch to take the job, which opened up the referee's position to Ed Smith. "Ed Smith Named as Referee for Big Fight," *Albuquerque Evening Herald*, June 15, 1912, 1.

8. Lester Young Smith had been ill for more than a year. His mother and sister were with him when he died. "Lester Smith, Base Ball Writer Dead," *Chicago Evening American*, June 4, 1912, 1; "Ed Smith Named as Referee."

9. Ed Smith, who was en route to Las Vegas, did not learn of his son's death until later that afternoon. "Young Newspaper Man Dies Here," *Las Vegas Optic*, June 4, 1912.

Chapter 18

1. "A federal grand jury sworn in today will be asked to return an indictment against Jack Johnson on a charge of smuggling." "Johnson Charged with Smuggling Gems," *Albuquerque Evening Herald*, June 11, 1912, 1.

2. "Jack Johnson and Wife Are Indicted," *Santa Fe New Mexican*, June 21, 1912, 7.

3. "Discredit Talk of Stopping Go," *Chicago Tribune*, June 19, 1912, 14.

4. "Johnson Jab Wins Arrest Witness in Smuggling Case. Says the Champion Slammed Him," *Chicago Daily Tribune*, June 13, 1912, 4.

5. "Jack Johnson Knocks Out Negro Chauffeur," *Albuquerque Morning Journal*, July 26, 1912.

Chapter 19

1. "Abdul's Opinion," *Kansas City Star*, June 19, 1912, 2B.

2. The Turk told reporters that Flynn had stopped smoking cigarettes long before he came to Las Vegas. John E. Wray said otherwise in a sports column titled "A Trifle Forgetful" for the *St. Louis Post-Dispatch* in June, mentioning that Flynn had been photographed smoking and drinking during his training time in Arkansas in late April of 1912.

3. "Abdul the Turk Picks Jim Flynn," *Pueblo Star Journal*, June 28, 1912, 10.

4. "Confidence Rules Camps of Both Fighters at Las Vegas," *Albuquerque Evening Herald*, June 26, 1912, 6.

Chapter 20

1. "Jim Flynn Working to Get into Condition to Defeat Johnson," *Pueblo Chieftain*, May 19, 1912, 15.

2. "Johnson Stays Fat, but Derides Challengers," *Chicago Evening American*, June 4, 1912.

3. "Johnson Is Nearly as Fat as Jeffries Was When He Began Training for That Reno Fight," *Evening World*, June 15, 1912.

4. "Johnson's Expansion an Inch Less Than That of Jim Flynn," *Las Vegas Optic*, June 17, 1912, 2; "Johnson Is Nearly as Fat."

5. No one seemed bothered by the question of chest expansion, least of all Johnson. He wasn't planning to run around the boxing ring for two hours on July Fourth; he was fit. "Champion's Wind Excellent Despite High Altitude of Training Camp," *St. Louis Post-Dispatch*, June 25, 1912, 15.

Chapter 21

1. Johnson did not take Flynn seriously in 1907. "Johnson Promises to Stop Flynn in Tenth," *San Francisco Examiner*, November 2, 1907.

2. "Johnson Promises."

3. "Johnson Promises."

4. "When Flynn Cried Enough," *San Francisco Chronicle*, June 6, 1912, 5.

5. The fans jeered Johnson because he had told reporters five months before that he was going to marry a piano-playing white woman from Australia named Alma "Lola" Toy. Ward, *Unforgivable Blackness*, 88.

6. "Big Negro Has All the Best of Fireman," *Los Angeles Herald*, November 4, 1907.

7. Associated Press, November 4, 1907.

8. "Johnson Scores Knockout," *New York Times*, November 3, 1907, 7.

9. "Johnson Joked with Jim Flynn in First Fight," *St. Louis Post-Dispatch*, July 4, 1912, 12.

10. "When Jim Flynn First Met Johnson," *Pueblo Star-Journal*, June 9, 1912, 3.

Chapter 22

1. Ward, *Unforgivable Blackness*, 196.

2. Most of them were the elite of the Fourth Estate. Callon, "Boxing's Greatest Fiasco," 15.

3. W. W. [William Walter] "Bill" Naughton had already published two books on the subject: *Kings of the Queensberry Realm* and *Heavyweight Champions*.

4. "Tribute to Fay Young," *Chicago Defender*, November 14, 1953. 1.

5. "Johnson-Flynn Bout Regarded as a Joke," *New York Times*, June 23, 1912, C-9.

6. That may be why the newspaper enjoyed writing about the Fighting Dentist, Leach Cross.

7. "Leach Cross Beats Brown at Garden," *New York Times*, June 4, 1912, 10.

8. "I don't know why he didn't go," said Masterson's biographer Robert K. DeArment in a telephone conversation on April 9, 2014.

9. "It must have made 'Lil Artha' nervous at times." Callon, "Boxing's Greatest Fiasco," 12.

10. Bill Naughton worked chiefly for the *San Francisco Examiner*. He died two years after the Johnson-Flynn fight. He was sixty years old. Boxrec.com.

Chapter 23

1. "Keep the Town Clean Says Mayor," *Las Vegas Optic*, June 24, 1912, 1. "Mayor instructs police to arrest persons defiling streets and alleyways."

2. "Out of the weeds" is the admonition of Chief of Police Ben Coles. *Las Vegas Optic*, June 20, 1912. Taupert agrees. "The mayor says he means to have those weeds cut. If they are cut now, much avoidance in the late summer will be avoided."

3. "Fire Two Shots at Liquor Dealer," *Santa Fe New Mexican*, May 27. 1912, 2. The West was wilder than people thought.

4. "Las Vegas Woman Tries to Roast Herself Alive," *Albuquerque Morning Journal*, May 7, 1912.

5. George Demitriz was en route from San Francisco to New York. In the smoking car, Demitriz believed that some men who boarded the train were plotting to rob and kill him. "Italian on Santa Fe Train Goes Insane," *Santa Fe New Mexican*, July 3, 1912, 3.

Chapter 24

1. "Johnson to Defend Title Thursday," *Los Angeles Daily Times*, July 3, 1912, part 3, 2.

2. "Johnson Fights Fireman Today," *New York Herald*, July 4, 1912, 11.

3. "Johnson's Smile Appears," *Inter Ocean*, July 3, 1912, 4.

Chapter 25

1. "Curley Will Try to Land Rivers Wolgast Fight," *Albuquerque Evening Herald*, May 15, 1912, 6. Curley could not secure the Wolgast-Rivers bout. "Curley Returns from California," *Albuquerque Evening Herald*, June 10, 1912, 6.

2.   "Springs Boys to Open Battle at Las Vegas," *Colorado Springs Gazette*, June 15, 1912, 7.

3.   "Fitzsimmons Says Johnson Sure to Win," *Colorado Springs Gazette*, July 3, 1912, 7.

Chapter 26

1.   "Big Crowd Already on Ground at Las Vegas," *Colorado Springs Gazette*, July 2, 1912, 1.

2.   "In Reno, Jeffries and Johnson had declined to shake hands. Johnson smiled and Jeffries chewed gum." Hagar and Clifton, *Johnson-Jeffries*, 62.

3.   "Returned Local Fans Call Fight a Fiasco," *Colorado Springs Gazette*, July 6, 1912, 6.

Chapter 27

1.   On eight occasions during the abbreviated run of this heavily boosted combat, Ed Smith threatened to disqualify Flynn. Five times Smith "called" the champion for holding. Johnson's bear hug at close range robbed the chunky Flynn of the use of his most effective weapon, infighting. To tear himself free, Flynn resorted to head-butting. "A Hopeless White Hope," *New York Herald*, July 5, 1912, 13.

2.   Kent, *Great White Hopes*, 119.

3.   Apparently Johnson did not attempt to hit hard. He contented himself with a slow, scientific chopping, every blow finding its way through the barricade of gloves and elbows behind which Flynn was crouched. "State Police Stop Johnson-Flynn Bout," *New York Times*, July 5, 1912, 9.

4.   Only once in the nine rounds did Johnson show any wish to end the fight. And yet ringside opinion was unanimous: he could have put Flynn out any time he happened to fancy, whether in the first or the ninth round. "Repeated Warnings," *Cincinnati Enquirer*, July 5, 1912, 8.

5.   The black champion was declared the winner after eight and a fraction rounds of the foulest fighting ever seen under Marquess of Queensberry rules. There had been no knockdowns and few clean blows. Only billy-goat tactics from Flynn. "Johnson Wins, Police Stop Battle in Ninth," *Inter Ocean*, July 5, 1912, 9.

Chapter 28

1.   Ward, *Unforgivable Blackness*, 217.

2.   "Killed in Prizefight Row," *Kansas City Star*, July 4, 1912, 1.

3.   "He Was Just Celebrating," *Milwaukee Journal*, July 5, 1912, 11.

4.   "Mob Lynches Negro," *Cleveland Press*, July 6, 1912, 2.

5.   "Black Belt Delirium," *Chicago Tribune*, July 5, 1912.

6. "Through a Window," *Cincinnati Enquirer*, July 5, 1912, 8.

7. "Las Vegas Battle Is Fatal to Flagman," *Albuquerque Morning Journal*, July 3, 1912, 3.

8. "It was a big crowd that gathered yesterday afternoon on the shady side of the *Albuquerque Morning Journal* building. Horace Sherman called the rounds. Sherman has a voice that carried seven blocks and his enunciation is singularly close to correct. It pleased the more than two thousand people, Anglo-Americans, Spanish-Americans and a few colored people interested in the black champion." "Morning Journal Bulletins Heard by Thousands," *Albuquerque Morning Journal*, July 5, 1912, 8.

Chapter 29

1. Curley lost $15,000. Moreover, Las Vegas businessmen, who were expecting profits from the crowds, lost $10,000 in expected sales. "Fans Pull Out of Las Vegas," *Omaha World-Herald*, July 5, 1912, 16.

2. "Mrs. Jack Won $6,000," *Milwaukee Journal*, July 6, 1912, 12.

3. "I would have had him in a few more rounds. No one that Johnson fought has extended him as much as I did." "Feeling Fine Jim Wires Mother," *Pueblo Star-Journal*, July 5, 1912, 1.

4. Besides receiving a used car, Jim Flynn found himself in trouble following the fight. The Fireman learned that Mr. F. B. Ufer of Tulsa, Oklahoma, had filed a lawsuit against him. Ufer claimed that Flynn had borrowed a few hundred dollars from him some time back and refused to pay it back. Promoters Curley and O'Malley, and the First National Bank of Las Vegas, where the money belonging to the fight syndicate was said to be on deposit, were included in the action. Ufer attempted to get into his possession any money that might be coming to Flynn. *Las Vegas Optic*, July 5, 1912. Ufer is said to have been the manager for Carl Morris at one time.

5. To the astonishment of many, a few days following the fight, Charles O'Malley huddled with a handful of men in town who had showed an interest in bringing another bout to New Mexico. O'Malley had already wired Johnson and Al Palzer. The latter was an extra large–size drawing card. If satisfactory terms could be reached, the match would be on Labor Day. O'Malley coaxed the men who had lost money by buying stock in the Flynn-Johnson disaster. They could take a chance on one more battle to retrieve their losses. And of course the Panama Canal was for sale.

6. "Governor's Policy Gains Him the Condemnation of the State," *Las Vegas Optic*, July 5, 1912.

Chapter 30

1. Scott said Johnson had made appearances in Lufkin and Nacogdoches, where crowds came from miles around to shake his hand. Additional appearances scheduled in Hattiesburg and Meridian, Mississippi, had fallen through. Lucas, *Black Gladiator*, 186.

2. Raleigh *News & Observer*, June 11, 1946, 1.

3. Dr. W. F. Clark, attending physician at St. Agnes Hospital, said that Johnson died of internal injuries and shock. "Jack Johnson Dies Here of Auto Wreck Injuries," Raleigh *News & Observer*, June 11, 1946, 1.

4. Johnson's funeral was held in Chicago at the Pilgrim Baptist Church on South Indiana Avenue. At the graveside, in Graceland Cemetery, a reporter dared ask his widow, Johnson's third wife, just what it was she loved about her husband. "I loved him because of his courage. He faced the world unafraid. There wasn't anybody or anything he feared." Ward, *Unforgivable Blackness*, 448. No one knows for sure exactly why Etta took her life. DeCoy, *Big Black Fire*, 140; Roberts, *Papa Jack*, 227.

5. Flynn's knockout of Dempsey was not without controversy. Dempsey said he had walked into the ring cold and had injured his hand. Flynn flattened Dempsey three times within two minutes of the first round. Kahn, *Flame of Pure Fire*, 447.

6. The game heart of Fireman Jim Flynn, which carried him through fifty-six wins and during bruising ring battles, stopped beating on April 12, 1935. "Death Claims Jim Flynn Famous Pueblo Ringster by Sudden Heart Attack," *Pueblo Chieftain*, April 13, 1935, 9.

7. "Any man who knew Jim Flynn would expect him to meet death with his fists doubled till the skin was stretched white over the broken knuckles, jaw set, daring the Grim Reaper, scythe and all." "Flynn True to His Code," *Los Angeles Times*, April 13, 1935, 1A.

8. "Ed Smith, a hard-boiled professional and the principal in many throbbing dramas of the prize ring, wrestling mat and newspaper office, will be missed. A roly-poly pal, a cheery smile and a close-buttoned, tight-fitting black overcoat and cane were his trademarks." "Ed W. Smith, Vet Sports Editor, Dies in West at 67," *Chicago American*, February 24, 1936, 17.

9. Jack Curley probably was the most versatile and industrious promoter the United States ever saw. He backed anything if it might turn a profit. That included a tour in the US by the Vatican choir, a bullfight in Montana, dance marathons, six-day bicycle races, and a Wild West show. "Jack Curley Funeral Is Set for Tomorrow," *New York Herald Tribune*, July 13, 1937, 16. "500 Attend Rites for Jack Curley," *New York Times*, July 15, 1937.

10. Julyan, *Place Names of New Mexico*, 223.

11. "Fornoff Death Recalls Exploits of Famous Mounted Police Who Made Rustling Unhealthy," *Santa Fe New Mexican*, November 27, 1935, 1.

12. After his accident in the Indy 500 race, Arthur W. Greiner never raced again. He started a car dealership in Chicago that was not successful. He began to drink heavily and act bizarrely. In 1916, his family had him committed to a Milwaukee insane asylum due to a nervous breakdown. He was thirty-two years old when he died. Leerhsen, *Blood and Smoke*, 235. Greiner's funeral was held at the family residence on Lincoln Avenue in Chicago. "Greiner Dies at Sanitarium," *Chicago Tribune*, May 25, 1925, 20.

BIBLIOGRAPHY

Books

Arango, Polly E., Katherine Chilton, Lance Chilton, James Dudley, Nancy Neary, and Patricia Stelzner. *New Mexico: A New Guide to the Colorful State*. Albuquerque: University of New Mexico Press, 1984.

Aycock, Colleen, and Mark Scott. *The First Black Boxing Champions: Essays on Fighters of the 1800s to the 1920s*. With a contribution by Chris Cozzone. Jefferson, NC: McFarland, 2011.

Barton, George A. *My Lifetime in Sports*. Minneapolis: Olympic Press, 1957.

Batchelor, Denzil. *Jack Johnson and His Times*. London: Weidenfeld and Nicholson, 1956.

Boddy, Kasia. *Boxing: A Cultural History*. London: Reaktion Books, 2008.

Breslin, Jimmy. *Damon Runyon: A Life*. New York: Ticknor and Fields, 1991.

Bryan, Howard. *Wildest of the Wild West: True Tales of a Frontier Town on the Santa Fe Trail*. Santa Fe, NM: Clear Light, 1991.

Buckley, Christopher. *But Enough About You: Essays*. New York: Simon and Schuster, 2014.

Callon, Milton W. *Las Vegas, New Mexico: The Town That Wouldn't Gamble*. Las Vegas, NM: Las Vegas Publishing Company, 1962.

Cavanaugh, Jack. *Tunney: Boxing's Brainiest Champ and His Upset of the Great Jack Dempsey*. New York: Random House, 2006.

Cozzone, Chris, and Jim Boggio. *Boxing in New Mexico, 1868–1940*. Jefferson, NC: McFarland, 2013.

Cray, Ed, Jonathan Kotler, and Miles Beller. *American Datelines: One Hundred and Forty Major News Stories from Colonial Times to the Present*. New York: Facts on File, 1990.

DeArment, Robert K. *Bat Masterson: The Man and the Legend*. Norman: University of Oklahoma Press, 1989.

DeCoy, Robert H. *The Big Black Fire*. Los Angeles: Holloway House, 1969.

Durant, John. *The Heavyweight Champions*. New York: Hastings House, 1971.

Eig, Jonathan. *Ali: A Life*. Boston / New York: Houghton Mifflin Harcourt, 2017.

Farr, Finis. *Black Champion: The Life and Times of Jack Johnson*. Greenwich, CT: Fawcett, 1969.

Frisbee, Meg. *Counterpunch: The Cultural Battles over Heavyweight Prizefighting in the American West*. Seattle and London: University of Washington Press, 2016.

Garcia, Nasario. *Old Las Vegas: Hispanic Memories from the New Mexico Meadowlands*. Lubbock: Texas Tech University Press, 2005.

Gilmore, Al-Tony. *Bad Nigger! The National Impact of Jack Johnson*. Port Washington, NY: Kennikat Press, 1975.

Glasrud, Bruce A. *African American History in New Mexico: Portraits from Five Hundred Years*. Albuquerque: University of New Mexico Press, 2013.

Gorn, Elliott J., and Warren Goldstein. *A Brief History of American Sports*. New York: Hill and Wang, 1993.

Hagar, Ray, and Guy Clifton. *Johnson-Jeffries: Dateline Reno*. Vancouver, WA: Pediment, 2010.

Halpern, Daniel, and Joyce Carol Oates, eds. *Reading the Fights*. New York: Henry Holt, 1988.

Heinz, W. C., ed. *The Fireside Book of Boxing*. New York: Simon and Schuster, 1961.

Hornung, Chuck. *New Mexico's Rangers: The Mounted Police*. Mount Pleasant, SC: Arcadia, 2010.

Johnson, Jack. *Jack Johnson—in the Ring—and Out*. Chicago, IL: National Sport, 1927.

———. *Jack Johnson Is a Dandy: An Autobiography*. New York: Chelsea House, 1969.

———. *My Life and Battles*. Washington, DC: Potomac Books, 2009.

Julyan, Robert. *The Place Names of New Mexico*. Albuquerque: University of New Mexico Press, 1996.

Kahn, Roger. *A Flame of Pure Fire: Jack Dempsey and the Roaring '20s*. New York: Harcourt Brace, 1999.

Kent, Graeme. *The Great White Hopes: The Quest to Defeat Jack Johnson*. Stroud, UK: Sutton, 2009.

Kimball, George, and John Schulian, eds. *At the Fights: American Writers on Boxing*. New York: Library of America, 2012.

Lang, Arne K. *The Nelson-Wolgast Fight and the San Francisco Boxing Scene, 1900–1914*. McFarland, 2012.

Leerhsen, Charles. *Blood and Smoke: A True Tale of Mystery, Mayhem, and the Birth of the Indy 500*. New York: Simon and Schuster, 2013.

Logan, Rayford Whittington. *The Betrayal of the Negro from Rutherford B. Hayes to Woodrow Wilson*. New York: Macmillan, 1965.

Lucas, Bob. *Black Gladiator: A Biography of Jack Johnson*. New York: Dell, 1970.

Matejka, Adrian. *The Big Smoke*. New York: Penguin, 2013.

Melzer, Richard. *Buried Treasures*. Santa Fe, NM: Sunstone Press, 2007.

Norrell, Robert J. *The House I Live In: Race in the American Century*. Oxford, UK: Oxford University Press, 2005.

Oates, Joyce Carol. *On Boxing*. Garden City, NY: Dolphin/Doubleday, 1987.

Perrigo, Lynn. *Gateway to Glorieta: A History of Las Vegas, New Mexico*. Boulder, CO: Pruett, 1985.

Reichler, Joe. *The Baseball Encyclopedia: The Complete and Official Record of Major League Baseball*. New York: Macmillan, 1993.

Roberts, Randy. *Papa Jack: Jack Johnson and the Era of White Hopes*. New York: Free Press, 1983.

Rozen, Wayne A. *America on the Ropes: A Pictorial History of the Johnson-Jeffries Fight*. Binghamton, NY: Casey Press, 2004.

Runstedtler, Theresa. *Jack Johnson, Rebel Sojourner: Boxing in the Shadow of the Global Color Line*. Berkeley: University of California Press, 2013.

Smith, Toby. *Kid Blackie: Jack Dempsey's Colorado Days*. Ouray, CO: Wayfinder Press, 1987.

Spink, Alfred H. *The National Game*. 2nd ed. Carbondale: Southern Illinois University Press, 2000.

Stone, Elaine Murray. *Dorothy Day: Champion of the Poor*. New York / Mahwah, NJ: Paulist Press, 2004.

Sugar, Bert Randolph. *Boxing's Greatest Fighters*. Guilford, CT: Lyons Press, 2009.

Ward, Geoffrey C. *Unforgivable Blackness: The Rise and Fall of Jack Johnson*. New York: Alfred A. Knopf, 2004.

Journal and Magazine Articles

Callon, Milton W. "Boxing's Greatest Fiasco." *Denver Westerners Roundup* 28, no. 7 (September 1972).

Curley, Jack. "Memoirs of a Promoter." With Frank Graham. *The Ring* (1930–1934).

Hutchison, Phillip. "Hyping White Hopes: Press Agentry and Its Media Affiliations during the Era of Jack Johnson, 1908–1915." *Journal of Public Relations Research* 23, no 3 (2011): 325–48.

Kammer, David J. "TKO in Las Vegas: Boosterism and the Johnson-Flynn Fight." *New Mexico Historical Review* (October 1986).

Turner, Frederick. "History in Towns: Another Las Vegas, This One in New Mexico." *The Magazine: Antiques* (16 July 2009).

Wilson, Raymond. "Another White Hope Bites the Dust: The Jack Johnson-Jim Flynn Heavyweight Fight in 1912." *Montana: The Magazine of History* (January 1979).

Booklets

Historic Las Vegas, New Mexico: Along the Santa Fe Trail. Las Vegas, NM: Las Vegas Citizens' Committee for Historic Preservation, 2006.

Websites

Sports Writers Register by Bill Burgess, http://baseballguru.com/bburgess/
    analysisbburgess20.html.

Documentaries

Burns, Ken, dir. *Unforgivable Blackness: The Rise and Fall of Jack Johnson.* Washing-
    ton, DC: Public Broadcasting Service, Florentine Films, and WETA, 2005.

Plays

Sackler, Howard. *The Great White Hope: A Drama in Three Acts.* New York, Holly-
    wood, London, Toronto: Samuel French Incorporated, 1968.

Movies

Ritt, Martin, dir. *The Great White Hope.* Los Angeles: 20th Century Fox, 1970.

Newspapers

Albuquerque Evening Herald
Albuquerque Morning Journal
Atlanta Journal
Bryan Democrat (Ohio)
Buffalo Enquirer
Chicago American
Chicago Daily News
Chicago Daily Tribune
Chicago Defender
Chicago Evening American
Chicago Examiner
Cincinnati Enquirer
Cleveland Press
Clovis News (New Mexico)
Colorado Springs Gazette
Daily Call (South Dakota)
Denver Post
Evening World (New York)
Hot Springs Sentinel-Record (Arkansas)
Inter Ocean (Illinois)
Kansas City Star
Las Vegas Optic

Los Angeles Daily Times
Los Angeles Examiner
Los Angeles Times
Morning Telegraph (New York)
National Police Gazette
News & Observer (North Carolina)
New York Herald Tribune
New York Times
New York Tribune
Omaha World-Herald
Pasadena Star-News
Pittsburgh Post
Pueblo Chieftain
Pueblo Star-Journal
Rocky Mountain News (Colorado)
San Francisco Call
San Francisco Chronicle
San Francisco Examiner
Santa Fe New Mexican
Shreveport News (Louisiana)
Sporting News
St. Louis Post-Dispatch
Tacoma Daily Ledger
Trinidad Chronicle News (Colorado)
Wichita Beacon

INDEX